HEROES

HEROES

SECOND EDITION

21 True Stories of Courage and Honor—with Exercises for Developing Reading Comprehension and Critical Thinking Skills

Henry Billings

Melissa Billings

JAMESTOWN PUBLISHERS

a division of NTC/CONTEMPORARY PUBLISHING GROUP
Lincolnwood, Illinois USA

ISBN 0-89061-108-4

Published by Jamestown Publishers,
a division of NTC/Contemporary Publishing Group, Inc.
4255 West Touhy Avenue,
Lincolnwood (Chicago), Illinois 60712-1975, U.S.A.

7 8 9 10 11 12 13 14 15 113 09 08 07 06 05 04 03

CONTENTS

UNIT THREE

To the Student

Who or what is a hero? What makes someone a hero? Are all heroes famous, or are some just everyday people? And are all heroes even people?

You probably think you know the answers to these questions now, but after you read the articles in this book and think about the heroes and their acts of heroism, you may feel differently. The heroes in these stories were tested by events or circumstances and reacted in ways that made a difference in people's lives, sometimes at great risk to themselves. As you read, think about what you would have done in the same situations.

The articles all tell about actual events. As you read and enjoy them, you will also be developing your reading skills. *Heroes* is for students who already read fairly well but who want to read faster and to increase their understanding. If you complete the 21 lessons—reading the articles and completing the exercises—you will surely increase your reading speed and improve your reading comprehension and critical thinking skills. Also, because these exercises include items of the types often found on state and national tests, learning how to complete them will help you prepare for tests you may have to take.

How to Use This Book

About the Book. *Heroes* contains three units, each of which includes seven lessons. Each lesson begins with an article about a heroic person or a challenging event followed by a set of four reading comprehension exercises and a set of four critical thinking exercises. The reading comprehension exercises will help you understand the article. The critical thinking exercises will help you think about what you read and how it relates it to your own experience.

At the end of each lesson, you will also have the opportunity to give your personal response to some aspect of the article and then to assess how well you understood what you read.

The Sample Lesson.   Working through the sample lesson, the first lesson in the book, with your class or group will demonstrate how a lesson is organized. The sample lesson explains how to complete the exercises and score your answers. The correct answers for the sample exercises and sample scores are printed in lighter type. In some cases explanations of the correct answers are given. The explanations will help you understand how to think through these question types.

If you have any questions about how to complete the exercises or score them, this is the time to get the answers.

Working Through Each Lesson.   Begin each lesson by looking at the photographs and reading the captions. Before you read, predict what you think the article will be about. Then read the article.

Sometimes your teacher may decide to time your reading. Timing helps you keep track of and increase your reading speed. If you have been timed, enter your reading time in the box at the end of the lesson, use the Words-per-Minute Table at the end of the unit to find your reading speed, and record your speed on the Reading Speed graph for that unit.

Next complete the Reading Comprehension and Critical Thinking exercises. The directions for each exercise will tell you how to mark your answers. When you have finished all four Reading Comprehension exercises, use the answer key provided by your teacher to check your work. Follow the directions after each exercise to find your score. Record your Reading Comprehension scores on the graph at the end of the unit. Then check your answers to the Author's Approach, Summarizing and Paraphrasing, and Critical Thinking exercises. Fill in the Critical Thinking chart at the end of each unit with your evaluation of your work and comments about your progress.

At the end of each unit you will also complete a Compare/Contrast chart. The completed chart will help you see what the articles have in common. It will also give you an opportunity to explore your own ideas about heroes and heroism.

THE MAN IN THE WATER
Not an Ordinary Man

O n January 13, 1982, a severe snowstorm hit Washington, D.C. The temperature fell to the mid teens. Driving snow made it hard to see. Flights out of Washington's National Airport were delayed while snowplows cleared the runways. Air Florida Flight 90, with its 79 passengers, was no exception. It was originally scheduled to depart at 2:15 P.M. Clearing the runways, however, took over an hour. At 3:37, the pilot was finally allowed to move the plane into position for takeoff. But 15 other planes were lined up ahead of it. Another 20 minutes went by before Flight 90 could roll out onto the runway.

2   While Flight 90 was waiting for the runways to be plowed, the ice that had formed on its wings was removed. But new ice began to form immediately. As the pilot waited for the 15 other planes to take off, the ice grew heavier. Ice buildup on a plane's wings is dangerous. It makes the plane heavier and disturbs the normal flow of air over the wings. Despite the fresh layer of ice, Flight 90 roared down the runway when its turn came at 3:59 P.M.

A rescue helicopter lifts a survivor of the crash of Air Florida Flight 90 from the icy waters of the Potomac River in Washington, D.C.

3   As the jet took off, it shuddered. Something was wrong. It was not gaining altitude as it should. One of the passengers, who was also a pilot, said, "We're not going to make it."

4   Meanwhile, traffic on the Fourteenth Street Bridge over the Potomac River was heavy. It was rush hour, and the workers who lived outside the city were headed home. Suddenly the blue, green, and white form of an Air Florida 727 appeared out of the clouds. Flight 90 was going down, and it was heading straight for the crowded bridge. The motorists on the bridge could do nothing but watch in horror as the airplane fell from the sky and smashed across the northbound lane. The tops of several cars were sheared off. Four motorists were killed before the plane plunged into the frigid Potomac and broke in two.

5   Rescue workers arrived on the scene quickly. Their searchlights revealed a hideous sight. Many of the passengers could be seen still strapped in their seats at the bottom of the Potomac. Only six passengers were still alive. They clung to a piece of the tail section that stuck out of the water. One of the people was a balding man with a large mustache. He seemed to be more alert and less severely injured than any of the others.

6   Speed was essential if the six people were to be saved. A person can survive only a few minutes in such cold water. The rescue was made difficult by the fact that there was only enough room for one helicopter to get between the Fourteenth Street Bridge and another bridge nearby.

7   A rescue helicopter arrived and quickly lowered its lifeline and flotation ring to the balding man. The man grabbed it, but instead of using it himself, he passed it on to one of the other passengers. As that person was lifted out of the freezing water, the balding man fought to keep his grip on the tail section. His body temperature was dropping, and the numbing cold of the water was sapping his strength. When the rescue helicopter returned, the lifeline was again dropped to him. Bystanders watched in amazement as the man once again passed the lifeline on to someone else. For the second time, he was giving up a chance to save himself in order to allow another person to be saved.

8   After a nerve-racking 10 minutes, the three other passengers had been taken safely to the shore. Only the balding man was left in the river. But when the helicopter returned to pick him up, he was gone. He had been in the icy water too long.

9   For several days, the selfless hero was known simply as "the man in the water." No one knew who he was. But when the passenger list was compared with the description of the man, it was determined that he was Arland Williams, a 46-year-old bank examiner from Atlanta, Georgia.

Arland Williams began the flight as an ordinary passenger and became a hero in the waters of the Potomac River.

10   When Arland Williams boarded Flight 90, he was an ordinary person on an ordinary flight. There was nothing special about him. Even his mother described him as "just average." He was simply another face in the crowd.

11   Like anyone else, Arland Williams wanted to live. In fact, he always insisted on sitting in the back of the plane "because it's safer back there." But at 4:01 P.M. on a stormy January day, when the plane he was on slammed into a bridge and tumbled into the Potomac, Williams chose to risk his life to save the lives of others. We don't know what he was thinking when he found himself hanging on to the tail section of that broken airplane. But he must have known that the longer he stayed in the water the more certain it was that he would die. Yet he did stay in the cold, black water and pass his lifeline on to others.

12   The "man in the water" became a national hero. He had given up his life so that other people might live.

If you have been timed while reading this article, enter your reading time below. Then turn to the Words-per-Minute table on page 71 and look up your reading speed (words per minute). Enter your reading speed on the graph on page 72.

Reading Time: Sample Lesson

_____ : _____
Minutes   Seconds

A | Finding the Main Idea

One statement below expresses the main idea of the article. One statement is too general, or too broad. The other statement explains only part of the article; it is too narrow. Label the statements using the following key:

M—Main Idea   **B—Too Broad**   **N—Too Narrow**

_____M_____ 1. Arland Williams, an average person, became a hero when he died in the Potomac River because he twice passed his lifeline on to save others. [This is the *main idea*. It tells who the story is about and what he did.]

_____N_____ 2. Arland Williams died in the icy Potomac River after the plane he was on crashed on takeoff. [This statement is *too narrow*. It doesn't tell anything about Williams's heroism.]

_____B_____ 3. A bank examiner from Georgia became a hero when he died by putting the lives of others ahead of his own. [This statement is true, but it is *too broad*. It doesn't tell who the man was or exactly what he did.]

_____15_____ Score 15 points for a correct M answer.

_____10_____ Score 5 points for each correct B or N answer.

_____25_____ **Total Score:** Finding the Main Idea

B | Recalling Facts

How well do you remember the facts in the article? Put an X in the box next to the answer that correctly completes each statement about the article.

1. The plane crash took place in
   ☐ a. Florida.
   ☐ b. Atlanta.
   ☒ c. Washington, D.C.

2. Air Florida Flight 90 crashed into the Potomac River
   ☒ a. right after takeoff.
   ☐ b. 30 minutes after takeoff.
   ☐ c. as it was attempting to land.

3. Immediately after the crash, there were only
   ☐ a. two passengers alive.
   ☒ b. six passengers alive.
   ☐ c. five passengers alive.

4. Arland Williams died because he
   ☐ a. had suffered head injuries in the crash.
   ☐ b. did not know how to swim.
   ☒ c. had been in the icy water too long.

5. Arland Williams always insisted on sitting
   ☒ a. in the back of the plane.
   ☐ b. near the exit doors.
   ☐ c. in the front of the plane.

Score 5 points for each correct answer.

_____25_____ **Total Score:** Recalling Facts

C | Making Inferences

When you combine your own experience and information from a text to draw a conclusion that is not directly stated in that text, you are making an inference. Below are five statements that may or may not be inferences based on information in the article. Label the statements using the following key:

C—Correct Inference   **F—Faulty Inference**

___C___ 1. The crash of Air Florida Flight 90 was caused, at least in part, by the delayed takeoff. [This is a *correct* inference. Waiting in line for the other planes to take off allowed the ice to build up again on the wings.]

___F___ 2. If the rescue workers had arrived on the scene sooner, most of the 79 passengers could have been saved. [This is a *faulty* inference. The rescue workers did arrive quickly. Most of the passengers died on impact or within just a minute or two.]

___C___ 3. If two helicopters had been able to operate at the scene of the crash, Arland Williams would have been saved. [This is a *correct* inference. If one helicopter could save five out of six people, then two helicopters would probably have been able to rescue all six people.]

___F___ 4. Arland Williams's job prepared him to handle such an emergency. [This is a *faulty* inference. He was a bank examiner, not a rescue worker.]

___F___ 5. Arland Williams had always wanted to be a hero. [This is a *faulty* inference. Before the crash, Arland Williams was an ordinary person. He did not go out of his way to seek danger.]

Score 5 points for each correct answer.

___25___ **Total Score:** Making Inferences

D | Using Words Precisely

Each numbered sentence below contains an underlined word or phrase from the article. Following the sentence are three definitions. One definition is closest to the meaning of the underlined word. One definition is opposite or nearly opposite. Label those two definitions using the following key. Do not label the remaining definition.

C—Closest   **O—Opposite or Nearly Opposite**

1. <u>Despite</u> the fresh layer of ice, Flight 90 roared down the runway when its turn came at 3:59 P.M.

___C___ a. in spite of

_____ b. on the other hand

___O___ c. because of

2. Their searchlights revealed a <u>hideous</u> sight.

_____ a. strange

___O___ b. appealing

___C___ c. dreadful

3. Speed was <u>essential</u> if the six people were to be saved.

_____ a. impossible

___C___ b. necessary

___O___ c. unimportant

4. His body temperature was dropping, and the numbing cold of the water was <u>sapping</u> his strength.

___O___ a. restoring

___C___ b. draining

_____ c. freezing

5. But when the passenger list was compared with the description of the man, it was <u>determined</u> that he was Arland Williams, a 46-year-old bank examiner from Atlanta, Georgia.

_____O_____ a. remained uncertain

_____ b. written down

_____C_____ c. concluded

__15__	Score 3 points for each correct C answer.
__10__	Score 2 points for each correct O answer.
__25__	**Total Score:** Using Words Precisely

Enter the four total scores in the spaces below, and add them together to find your Reading Comprehension Score. Then record your score on the graph on page 73.

Score	Question Type	Sample Lesson
25	Finding the Main Idea	
25	Recalling Facts	
25	Making Inferences	
25	Using Words Precisely	
100	**Reading Comprehension Score**	

Author's Approach

Put an X in the box next to the correct answer.

1. What does the author mean by the statement "But when the helicopter returned to pick him up, he was gone"?
☐ a. Someone had rescued the balding man.
☒ b. The balding man had fallen into the water and drowned.
☐ c. The balding man had mysteriously disappeared.

2. The main purpose of the first paragraph is to
☒ a. explain the impact of the weather on Flight 90.
☐ b. inform the reader about the effect of severe weather on air travel.
☐ c. convey a fearful mood.

3. Which of the following statements from the article best describes Arland Williams?
☒ a. "Williams chose to risk his life to save the lives of others."
☐ b. "Like anyone else, Arland Williams wanted to live."
☐ c. "He was simply another face in the crowd."

4. The author probably wrote this article in order to
☐ a. describe the passengers' terrifying experience on Flight 90.
☐ b. identify the "man in the water."
☒ c. relate the story of an ordinary man who became a hero.

__4__	Number of correct answers

Record your personal assessment of your work on the Critical Thinking Chart on page 74.

Summarizing and Paraphrasing

Put an X in the box next to the correct answer for question 1. Follow the directions provided for the other questions.

1. Below are summaries of the article. Choose the summary that says all the most important things about the article but in the fewest words.

☐ a. After his plane crashed, Arland Williams became a hero. [This summary doesn't tell why Williams was a hero.]

☒ b. After Flight 90 crashed into the Potomac River, passenger Arland Williams gave up his own life to save others. [This summary contains all the most important information in the article.]

☐ c. After Air Florida Flight 90 crashed into the Potomac and broke in two, Arland Williams died after repeatedly passing a helicopter's lifeline to other passengers. [This summary contains important information from the article but includes too many details.]

2. Read the following statement about the article. Then read the paraphrase of that statement. Choose the reason that best tells why the paraphrase does not say the same thing as the statement.

   Statement: Although ice had been removed earlier from the wings of the airplane, a fresh layer had formed while the plane sat waiting on the runway.

   Paraphrase: While the plane sat on the runway, all of the ice on its wings was removed.

☐ a. Paraphrase says too much.

☐ b. Paraphrase doesn't say enough.

☒ c. Paraphrase doesn't agree with the statement about the article. [The paraphrase contradicts the statement; the ice formed while the plane sat on the runway.]

3. Choose the best one-sentence paraphrase for the following sentence from the article:
   "As that person was lifted out of the freezing water, the balding man fought to keep his grip on the tail section."

☐ a. The balding man struggled to hold on as he was lifted out of the water. [This paraphrase is incorrect; the balding man was not lifted out of the water.]

☐ b. After someone was lifted from the water, the tail section moved and the balding man had trouble holding on to it. [This paraphrase is incorrect; the tail section did not move.]

☒ c. The balding man's strength continued to drain as another passenger was lifted to safety. [This sentence correctly paraphrases the sentence from the article.]

___3___ Number of correct answers

Record your personal assessment of your work on the Critical Thinking Chart on page 74.

Critical Thinking

Put an X in the box next to the correct answer for questions 2, 3, and 4. Follow the directions provided for the other questions.

1. For each statement below, write O if it expresses an opinion and write F if it expresses a fact.

___O___ a. Arland Williams was an ordinary man.[This sentence is an opinion because it presents a view or judgment.]

___F___ b. Williams always sat in the back of the plane because he believed he would be safer there. [This sentence states a fact—something that can be proved.]

___O___ c. Traveling by airplane is more dangerous than traveling by car. [This sentence is an opinion because it expresses a belief.]

2. From the article, you can predict that if Arland Williams had been lifted out of the water first,

☒ a. many of the other passengers clinging to the tail section would have died. [This is a valid prediction because Williams was instrumental in their rescue.]

☐ b. he would have jumped back in to save the other passengers.

☐ c. he would have died anyway.

3. What was the effect of Williams's handing the lifeline to the other passengers?

☐ a. The other passengers died.

☒ b. The other passengers lived. [This is the correct effect. The other passengers lived because Williams gave them the lifeline.]

☐ c. Williams was less severely injured.

4. What was the cause of the crash of Flight 90?

☒ a. A layer of ice had formed on the wings and not been removed. [This is the correct cause. Ice on the wings made the plane too heavy to gain enough altitude.]

☐ b. The plane hit several cars on a bridge.

☐ c. Driving snow made flying difficult.

5. Which paragraphs from the article provide evidence that supports your answer to question 4? _____2 and 3_____ [These paragraphs explain the danger of ice buildup on an airplane's wings.]

_____7_____ Number of correct answers

Record your personal assessment of your work on the Critical Thinking Chart on page 74.

Personal Response

Why do you think Arland Williams passed the lifeline to the other passengers? [Your answer should explain what might have motivated Williams's heroic deed.]

_____

_____

_____

_____

Self-Assessment

While reading the article, _____ was the easiest for me to understand. [Identify a word, idea, or concept that was easiest for you.]

_____

_____

_____

_____

Self-Assessment

To get the most out of the Critical Reading series program, you need to take charge of your own progress in improving your reading comprehension and critical thinking skills. Here are some of the features that help you work on those essential skills.

Reading Comprehension Exercises.   Complete these exercises immediately after reading the article. They help you recall what you have read, understand the stated and implied main ideas, and add words to your working vocabulary.

Critical Thinking Skills Exercises.   These exercises help you focus on the author's approach and purpose, recognize and generate summaries and paraphrases, and identify relationships between ideas.

Personal Response and Self-assessment.   Questions in this category help you relate the articles to your personal experience and give you the opportunity to evaluate your understanding of the information in that lesson.

Compare and Contrast Charts.   At the end of each unit you will complete a Compare and Contrast chart. The completed chart helps you see what the articles have in common and gives you an opportunity to explore your own ideas about the topics discussed in the articles.

The Graphs.   The graphs and charts at the end of each unit enable you to keep track of your progress. Check your graphs regularly with your teacher. Decide whether your progress is satisfactory or whether you need additional work on some skills. What types of exercises are you having difficulty with? Talk with your teacher about ways to work on the skills in which you need the most practice.

UNIT ONE

WILMA RUDOLPH
Against the Odds

Wilma Rudolph streaks across the finish line to win the 400-meter relay in the 1960 Olympics in Rome, Italy.

The moment had come. The runners finished their warm-up exercises. On that August day in 1960, everyone in the Olympic Stadium watched as the fastest women in the world prepared to compete in the 400-meter relay.

2   When the pistol sounded, the first runners dashed from their starting blocks. There were four women on each team, and each woman had to run 100 meters—one "leg" of the race. As the first runners completed their leg, each had to pass a baton, or stick, to the next runner on her team. It was the fourth runner for each team who would carry the baton across the finish line.

3   The Germans got off to a good start, but the Americans were faster. After the first three legs, the Americans led the Germans by about two yards.

4   The last runner for the United States was a young black woman named Wilma Rudolph. As the third American raced toward her, Wilma readied herself for the pass. The audience watched tensely as the baton was passed to Wilma. Then a gasp

went up from the crowd. It was a bad pass. Wilma was forced to stop to pick up the fumbled baton. As she did so, Germany's Jutta Heine went flying by to take the lead.

5   America's only hope now was that Wilma Rudolph could somehow muster the strength and the speed to catch the fleet German runner. Most people did not know it, but this was not the first time Wilma had faced overwhelming odds.

6   From the moment she was born in 1940, Wilma Glodean Rudolph had to fight hard. She weighed just four and a half pounds at birth. Her parents feared she would not survive. But she did survive, and slowly her strength grew. After a few weeks, the Rudolphs were able to take her home. There she joined her 15 brothers and sisters in their rented cottage in Clarksville, Tennessee.

7   For a while Wilma's health continued to improve. But when she was four years old she was stricken with double pneumonia and scarlet fever. Again her life was in danger, but again Wilma pulled through. That time, however, she was left with a paralyzed left leg.

8   Doctors in the small town of Clarksville told Mrs. Rudolph that her daughter would never walk again, but Mrs. Rudolph refused to believe it.

Instead, she carried her small daughter to the bus terminal and took her on a 45-mile bus trip to a clinic in Nashville.

9   At the clinic, doctors examined Wilma's leg closely. After many tests, they came to a conclusion. They made no promises, but told Mrs. Rudolph that there was one hope. If Wilma could have special heat and water massages at the clinic every day, she might someday be able to walk again.

10   Mrs. Rudolph could not take Wilma to the clinic every day. The family was poor, the clinic was a long distance away, and there were 15 other children to care for at home. Besides, Mrs. Rudolph had to work six days a week as a maid to help support the family.

11   Mrs. Rudolph decided that there was only one thing to do. She must learn to give the special massages to Wilma herself. From the doctors, she learned the special massage technique. For the next two years, Wilma's mother massaged her daughter's leg every day. Usually she sat rubbing the leg until long after little Wilma had fallen asleep. Three of the older Rudolph children also learned to give the massage. Soon Wilma was having four treatments a day. In addition, on the one day each week that Mrs. Rudolph did not have to work, she took Wilma to the Nashville clinic for extra treatment.

12   For almost two years the massages seemed to do no good. Wilma spent all her time confined to a chair or bed. There was no money in the family to buy a wheelchair. By the time she was six, though, Wilma felt strong enough to try walking. She would hop along for a short distance, and then her weak leg would buckle and she would fall. But she did not give up. Determined to overcome her handicap, she kept trying. Gradually she was able to go farther and farther before

Wilma Rudolph wearing one of the three gold medals she won at the 1960 Olympics

collapsing. By the time she was eight years old, Wilma could walk with the help of a leg brace. A special shoe was made to support the weak ankle of her left leg. And so, for the first time, Wilma was able to go to school.

13 But just barely being able to walk was not enough for Wilma. She kept exercising to increase the strength of her left leg. By the time she was 11, Wilma could walk without the brace or the special shoe. When she was 13, she was chosen for the high school basketball team. And at 15 she was averaging 32.1 points per game and was selected for the all-state team.

14 It was during a basketball game that Wilma was discovered by Ed Temple, track coach for Tennessee State University. He thought he saw in her a great runner. He was not wrong. With his encouragement, in her senior year of high school Wilma applied to Tennessee State University. She was accepted, and became the first person in her family to attend college.

15 Once in college, Wilma set her sights on the 1960 Olympics. Early in 1960, however, she went into the hospital. Her tonsils had to be removed. The operation interrupted her training schedule, but that didn't stop Wilma. Three weeks after the operation, she was back out on the track practicing. When it came time for the Americans to go to Rome for the 1960 Olympic Games, Wilma was part of the team.

16 So, as Wilma ran after Germany's Jutta Heine on that August day during the last leg of the 400-meter relay, she once again found the strength to beat the odds. Quickly she closed the gap between herself and Heine. Then, in the final seconds of the race, Wilma pulled ahead. She led the Americans to a gold medal and a new world record.

17 Wilma Rudolph won three gold medals during the 1960 Olympics. She won the 100-meter dash by three yards, and tied the world record for that event. She also set a new Olympic record when she won the 200-meter dash. She was the first American woman to win three gold medals in track in one Olympic year. The sickly little girl who spent four years as an invalid and another three years in a leg brace had become the fastest female runner in the world. 🍃

If you have been timed while reading this article, enter your reading time below. Then turn to the Words-per-Minute Table on page 71 and look up your reading speed (words per minute). Enter your reading speed on the graph on page 72.

Reading Time: Lesson 1

_____ : _____
Minutes   Seconds

A | Finding the Main Idea

One statement below expresses the main idea of the article. One statement is too general, or too broad. The other statement explains only part of the article; it is too narrow. Label the statements using the following key:

M—Main Idea   **B—Too Broad**   **N—Too Narrow**

___N___ 1. Though doctors said that Wilma Rudolph would never walk again, through courage and hard work she overcame her handicap.

___B___ 2. Wilma Rudolph fought and overcame a serious physical handicap and went on to win three Olympic gold medals and become the world's fastest female runner.

___M___ 3. Though she began life as a sickly child, Wilma Rudolph became a great athlete.

_____ Score 15 points for a correct M answer.

_____ Score 5 points for each correct B or N answer.

_____ **Total Score:** Finding the Main Idea

B | Recalling Facts

How well do you remember the facts in the article? Put an X in the box next to the answer that correctly completes each statement about the article.

1. In the 400-meter relay at the 1960 Olympic Games, Wilma Rudolph ran the
   - ☐ a. first leg.
   - ☐ b. third leg.
   - ☒ c. last leg.

2. After the bad baton pass, the German team
   - ☒ a. took the lead.
   - ☐ b. increased its lead by two yards.
   - ☐ c. won the race despite a fast finish by Wilma Rudolph.

3. When Wilma Rudolph was born, her parents
   - ☐ a. thought she had scarlet fever.
   - ☒ b. feared she would not survive.
   - ☐ c. knew she would one day be a great athlete.

4. The special treatment that doctors suggested for Wilma Rudolph's leg was
   - ☒ a. daily massages.
   - ☐ b. warm blankets.
   - ☐ c. a leg brace.

5. The first sport in which Wilma became involved in high school was
   - ☐ a. field hockey.
   - ☐ b. track.
   - ☒ c. basketball.

_____ Score 5 points for each correct answer.

_____ **Total Score:** Recalling Facts

C | Making Inferences

When you combine your own experience and information from a text to draw a conclusion that is not directly stated in that text, you are making an inference. Below are five statements that may or may not be inferences based on information in the article. Label the statements using the following key:

C—Correct Inference   **F—Faulty Inference**

_____ 1. If Wilma Rudolph had been born strong and healthy she would not have become a great runner.

_____ 2. Part of the credit for Wilma Rudolph's success belongs to her mother and her family.

_____ 3. The doctors in the town in which Wilma lived as a child were not as knowledgeable about medicine as were the doctors at the clinic.

_____ 4. Wilma did not compete in any more races after the 1960 Olympics.

_____ 5. Wilma Rudolph was the fastest of the four American runners in the 400-meter relay race.

Score 5 points for each correct answer.

_____ **Total Score:** Making Inferences

D | Using Words Precisely

Each numbered sentence below contains an underlined word or phrase from the article. Following the sentence are three definitions. One definition is closest to the meaning of the underlined word. One definition is opposite or nearly opposite. Label those two definitions using the following key. Do not label the remaining definition.

C—Closest   **O—Opposite or Nearly Opposite**

1. The audience watched <u>tensely</u> as the baton was passed to Wilma.

    _____ a. in terror

    _____ b. anxiously

    _____ c. calmly

2. America's only hope now was that Wilma Rudolph could somehow muster the strength and the speed to catch the <u>fleet</u> German runner.

    _____ a. thin

    _____ b. slow

    _____ c. swift

3. Wilma spent all her time <u>confined</u> to a chair or bed.

    _____ a. free to move

    _____ b. reclining on

    _____ c. restricted to

4. She would hop along for a short distance, and then her weak leg would <u>buckle</u> and she would fall.

    _____ a. give way

    _____ b. straighten up

    _____ c. become sprained

5. The sickly little girl who spent four years as an <u>invalid</u> and another three years in a leg brace had become the fastest female runner in the world.

_____ a. depressed person

_____ b. disabled person

_____ c. healthy person

_____ Score 3 points for each correct C answer.

_____ Score 2 points for each correct O answer.

_____ **Total Score:** Using Words Precisely

Enter the four total scores in the spaces below, and add them together to find your Reading Comprehension Score. Then record your score on the graph on page 73.

Score	Question Type	Lesson 1
_____	Finding the Main Idea	
_____	Recalling Facts	
_____	Making Inferences	
_____	Using Words Precisely	
_____	**Reading Comprehension Score**	

Author's Approach

Put an X in the box next to the correct answer.

1. What does the author mean by the statement "this was not the first time Wilma had faced overwhelming odds"?

☐ a. This was not the first time Wilma had come from behind to win a race.

☐ b. Wilma would not win the race.

☐ c. Wilma had had to overcome great difficulties before.

2. Based on the statement from the article, "but just barely being able to walk was not enough for Wilma," you can conclude that the author wants the reader to think that Wilma

☐ a. wouldn't be satisfied until she could walk normally.

☐ b. didn't think she would ever walk again.

☐ c. felt sorry for herself.

3. Choose the statement below that best describes the author's position in paragraph 11.

☐ a. Wilma's mother did everything she could to help her daughter fight the paralysis.

☐ b. Mrs. Rudolph was too poor to take Wilma to the Nashville clinic every day.

☐ c. Wilma's brothers and sisters resented the attention their sister received from their mother.

_____ Number of correct answers

Record your personal assessment of your work on the Critical Thinking Chart on page 74.

CRITICAL THINKING

Summarizing and Paraphrasing

Put an X in the box next to the correct answer for question 1. Follow the directions provided for the other questions.

1. Below are summaries of the article. Choose the summary that says all the most important things about the article but in the fewest words.

☐ a. Wilma Rudolph came from behind to win a gold medal in the 1960 Olympics.

☐ b. Wilma Rudolph overcame poverty and physical handicaps to become the world's fastest woman.

☐ c. After Wilma Rudolph's leg became paralyzed, her doctors said that she would never walk again. However, Wilma overcame the odds and became a great runner.

2. Reread paragraph 12 in the article. Below, write a summary of the paragraph in no more than 25 words.

_____

_____

_____

_____

Reread your summary and decide if the summary covers important parts of the paragraph. Next, decide how to shorten the summary to 15 words or less without leaving out any essential information. Write this summary below.

_____

_____

_____

3. Choose the best one-sentence paraphrase for the following sentence from the article:

"When the pistol sounded, the first runners dashed from their starting blocks."

☐ a. At the signal, the team runners began to race down the field.

☐ b. The sound of a gun startled the runners.

☐ c. Some of the runners left their starting positions too soon.

_____ Number of correct answers

Record your personal assessment of your work on the Critical Thinking Chart on page 74.

Critical Thinking

Put an X in the box next to the correct answer for questions 3 and 4. Follow the directions provided for the other questions.

1. For each statement below, write O if it expresses an opinion and write F if it expresses a fact.

_____ a. Doctors in Clarksville, Tennessee, told Mrs. Rudolph that Wilma would never walk again.

_____ b. Wilma Rudolph is the greatest female runner in American history.

_____ c. In 1960, Wilma was the fastest female runner in the world.

2. Choose from the letters below to correctly complete the following statement. Write the letters on the lines.

In the article, _____ and _____ are alike.

a. Wilma Rudolph

b. Jutta Heine

c. Mrs. Rudolph

3. What was the cause of Wilma's paralysis?

☐ a.   her low birth weight

☐ b.   her family's poverty

☐ c.   an attack of double pneumonia and scarlet fever

4. How is Wilma Rudolph an example of a hero?

☐ a.   She refused to give up on herself or her dreams.

☐ b.   She led her team to a gold medal victory in the 1960 Olympics.

☐ c.   She was the first person in her family to attend college.

5. Which paragraphs from the article provide evidence that supports your answer to question 2?

_____

_____ Number of correct answers

Record your personal assessment of your work on the Critical Thinking Chart on page 74.

Personal Response

How do you think Wilma Rudolph felt when she was able to walk to school for the first time?

_____

_____

_____

Self-Assessment

What concepts or ideas from the article were difficult?

_____

_____

_____

_____

Which were easy?

_____

_____

_____

_____

DIANA GOLDEN
Go for the Gold

Olympic gold medalist Diana Golden zooms down a Colorado mountainside.

Diana Golden was 12 years old when she found out she had cancer. She was walking home one day after playing in the snow when her right leg simply gave out. Doctors diagnosed the problem as bone cancer. They recommended amputating her leg above the knee.

2 When Diana heard the news, she asked the first question that popped into her mind: "Will I still be able to ski?"

3 "When the doctors said yes," she later recalled, "I figured it wouldn't be too bad."

4 That attitude typified Diana's outlook on life. Losing a leg would devastate most children, but Diana refused to dwell on the negative. Instead, she told people again and again that it was no big deal. "Losing a leg?" she'd say. "It's nothing. A body part."

5 Most of all, Diana didn't want to let cancer stop her from doing what she loved. And what she loved was skiing. Diana had been on skis since the age of five. Her home in Lincoln, Massachusetts, was just a couple of hours from New Hampshire's Cannon Mountain, where her family owned a vacation house. After the amputation, Diana worked hard to get back to the mountain. "I always skied,

and I intended to keep on skiing. There was never any question in my mind about that," she declared. Seven months after losing her leg, Diana met her goal. She was back out on the slopes.

6   Skiing wasn't quite the same with just one leg, but Diana made the best of it. She used outriggers—special ski poles that were like crutches with small skis attached. She learned to go faster on one leg than most people could go on two. In high school, Diana became a member of her school's ski racing team. And in 1979, when she was just 17, she earned a spot on the U.S. Disabled Ski Team.

7   After high school, Diana Golden went on to Dartmouth College. There she saw how top two-legged skiers trained. Determined not to be left behind, Diana began training with the Dartmouth team. When they ran around the track, she followed them on crutches. When they ran up and down the steps of the football stadium, she went up and down the steps too—by hopping. "I had to adapt," she later explained. "I was an athlete. I had one leg, which meant I had to do it differently."

8   In 1982, Diana entered her first international ski race. She went to the World Handicapped Championships in Norway, where she won the downhill competition. She came in second in the giant slalom.

9   Soon after that, though, Diana quit skiing. She didn't like the fact that people thought of her as "the inspirational girl who overcame cancer." So for two years she did no racing at all. Then, in 1984, she went skiing with a friend. While on the mountain, she saw gates set out for a ski race. That did it; the old desire came flooding back. Diana decided to return to ski racing. Only this time, she didn't just want to be a top disabled skier. She wanted to be a top skier, period. She wanted to prove herself against racers with two legs, not just those with one. As she put it, "I wanted to be recognized as a top-notch athlete, as the best in the world."

10   In order to be the best, Diana had to give up her outriggers. She taught herself to ski with regular ski poles. That meant learning a new way of balancing herself. It also meant lifting lots of weights to strengthen her stomach, arms, and leg. With regular poles, she was able to reach speeds of 65 miles per hour.

11   Meanwhile, Diana still competed in ski races for the disabled. In fact, within a year of returning to the sport, she won gold medals in four big international races. But she also skied against nondisabled athletes. She lobbied to get the United States Ski Association (USSA) to welcome disabled skiers into its regular races.

12   Her efforts led to passage of the USSA "Golden Rule." This rule reserved slots for

Diana Golden poses after winning the World Disabled Ski Championship.

top disabled skiers early in a race. No longer would Diana and other disabled skiers have to wait until the end of the day to make their runs. Now they were allowed to go after the top 15 regular racers. That way they could ski the course before it became too rough.

13 In 1986, Diana won the Beck Award, which is given to the best American racer in international skiing. The next year, she placed 10th in a race against some of the best nondisabled skiers in the country. And in 1988, she was named *Ski Racing* magazine's U.S. Female Alpine Skier of the Year.

14 One of Diana's biggest thrills came in 1988. That was the year she went to the Olympic Games. Diana won the gold medal in the disabled giant slalom event. The U.S. Olympic Committee named her its Female Skier of the Year.

15 As a result of her courage and determination, Diana has changed the way the world looks at disabled athletes. Instead of seeing them as sad and pitiable, people have begun to see them as strong and competent. "Everyone has some kind of 'disability,'" Diana says. "It's what we do with our abilities that matters."

16 Diana was proud to have made a difference. But it wasn't something she had intended. "I never went into it to change things for the disabled," she said. "It was a quest within myself." Still, she acknowledged that her quest opened doors for others. "It was in the process of chasing my dreams that things happened...."

17 In 1990, Diana retired from racing for good. By then, she had won 29 gold medals as a disabled skier. She was recognized as one of the greatest skiers the United States has ever produced. Best of all, she had done what she set out to do. People no longer thought, "Diana Golden, disabled skier." Instead, they simply thought, "Diana Golden, great skier."

If you have been timed while reading this article, enter your reading time below. Then turn to the Words-per-Minute Table on page 71 and look up your reading speed (words per minute). Enter your reading speed on the graph on page 72.

Reading Time: Lesson 2

_____ : _____
Minutes   Seconds

A Finding the Main Idea

One statement below expresses the main idea of the article. One statement is too general, or too broad. The other statement explains only part of the article; it is too narrow. Label the statements using the following key:

M—Main Idea   **B—Too Broad**   **N—Too Narrow**

_____ 1. Doctors amputated Diana Golden's leg after they discovered that she had bone cancer.

_____ 2. After losing a leg to cancer, Diana Golden became a champion skier in both disabled and nondisabled events.

_____ 3. Diana Golden is one of the greatest skiers the United States has ever produced.

_____ Score 15 points for a correct M answer.

_____ Score 5 points for each correct B or N answer.

_____ **Total Score:** Finding the Main Idea

B Recalling Facts

How well do you remember the facts in the article? Put an X in the box next to the answer that correctly completes each statement about the article.

1. Diana Golden found out that she had cancer when she was

☐ a. 5 years old.

☐ b. 12 years old.

☐ c. 17 years old.

2. Diana learned to ski on one leg using

☐ a. regular ski poles.

☐ b. crutches.

☐ c. outriggers.

3. After winning the downhill competition in her first international ski race, Diana

☐ a. quit skiing for two years.

☐ b. began training with the Dartmouth ski team.

☐ c. earned a spot on the U.S. Disabled Ski Team.

4. When Diana returned to ski racing, she

☐ a. only competed in races for the disabled.

☐ b. competed in races against disabled and nondisabled skiers.

☐ c. only competed in races for the nondisabled.

5. In 1987, Diana raced against some of the country's best nondisabled skiers and

☐ a. won the Beck Award.

☐ b. was named Female Alpine Skier of the Year.

☐ c. placed 10th.

Score 5 points for each correct answer.

_____ **Total Score:** Recalling Facts

C | Making Inferences

When you combine your own experience and information from a text to draw a conclusion that is not directly stated in that text, you are making an inference. Below are five statements that may or may not be inferences based on information in the article. Label the statements using the following key:

C—Correct Inference   **F—Faulty Inference**

_____ 1. Disabled skiers do not have as much athletic ability as nondisabled skiers.

_____ 2. When Diana Golden trained with the Dartmouth ski team, she had to work harder than the two-legged skiers.

_____ 3. Diana loved to compete.

_____ 4. Most people thought Diana Golden was sad and pitiable because of her disability.

_____ 5. Diana retired from ski racing because she had lost interest in the sport.

Score 5 points for each correct answer.

_____ **Total Score:** Making Inferences

D | Using Words Precisely

Each numbered sentence below contains an underlined word or phrase from the article. Following the sentence are three definitions. One definition is closest to the meaning of the underlined word. One definition is opposite or nearly opposite. Label those two definitions using the following key. Do not label the remaining definition.

C—Closest   **O—Opposite or Nearly Opposite**

1. Losing a leg would <u>devastate</u> most children.

_____ a. terrify

_____ b. encourage

_____ c. greatly sadden

2. "I had to <u>adapt</u>," she later explained.

_____ a. make some adjustments

_____ b. refuse to change

_____ c. fight hard

3. She <u>lobbied</u> to get the United States Ski Association (USSA) to welcome disabled skiers into its regular races.

_____ a. voted

_____ b. used her influence

_____ c. did not act

4. Instead of seeing them as sad and pitiable, people have begun to see them as strong and <u>competent</u>.

_____ a. powerful

_____ b. unfit

_____ c. well-qualified

5. She acknowledged that her <u>quest</u> opened doors for others.

_____ a. mission

_____ b. positive attitude

_____ c. inactivity

_____ Score 3 points for each correct C answer.

_____ Score 2 points for each correct O answer.

_____ **Total Score:** Using Words Precisely

Enter the four total scores in the spaces below, and add them together to find your Reading Comprehension Score. Then record your score on the graph on page 73.

Score	Question Type	Lesson 2
_____	Finding the Main Idea	
_____	Recalling Facts	
_____	Making Inferences	
_____	Using Words Precisely	
_____	**Reading Comprehension Score**	

Author's Approach

Put an X in the box next to the correct answer.

1. Which of the following statements from the article best describes Diana Golden?
   - ☐ a. "Diana refused to dwell on the negative."
   - ☐ b. "Diana had been on skis since the age of five."
   - ☐ c. "She learned to go faster on one leg than most people could go on two."

2. From the statements below, choose the one that you believe the author would agree with.
   - ☐ a. Diana lacked confidence.
   - ☐ b. Diana never felt sorry for herself.
   - ☐ c. Diana should have competed only in disabled ski races.

3. What does the author imply by saying that Diana "didn't like the fact that people thought of her as 'the inspirational girl who overcame cancer'"?
   - ☐ a. Diana thought people pitied her because she was disabled.
   - ☐ b. Diana didn't want people to know that she had had cancer.
   - ☐ c. Diana wanted to be respected for her ability, not for her disability.

4. The author probably wrote this article in order to
   - ☐ a. describe the events in an international ski competition.
   - ☐ b. inform readers about disabled skiers.
   - ☐ c. inspire readers with Diana's courage.

_____ Number of correct answers

Record your personal assessment of your work on the Critical Thinking Chart on page 74.

CRITICAL THINKING

Summarizing and Paraphrasing

Put an X in the box next to the correct answer for questions 2 and 3. Follow the directions provided for the other question.

1. Look for the important ideas and events in paragraphs 6 and 7. Summarize those paragraphs in one or two sentences.

_____

_____

_____

_____

2. Below are summaries of the article. Choose the summary that says all the most important things about the article but in the fewest words.

☐ a. After Diana Golden lost a leg to cancer, she learned to ski on one leg.

☐ b. Diana Golden won many medals as a disabled skier. She changed the way people look at disabled athletes.

☐ c. After losing a leg to cancer, Diana Golden worked hard to become a championship skier and a respected athlete.

3. Choose the sentence that correctly restates the following sentence from the article:

"Determined not to be left behind, Diana began training with the Dartmouth team."

☐ a. Diana trained as hard as she could because she didn't want to come in last.

☐ b. Diana worked hard to keep up with the other members of the ski team.

☐ c. Diana trained hard because she wanted to be the best skier on the team.

_____ Number of correct answers

Record your personal assessment of your work on the Critical Thinking Chart on page 74.

Critical Thinking

Put an X in the box next to the correct answer for questions 1, 2, and 5. Follow the directions provided for the other questions.

1. Which of the following statements from the article is an opinion rather than a fact?

☐ a. "Diana had been on skis since the age of five."

☐ b. "'It's what we do with our abilities that matters.'"

☐ c. "Diana won the gold medal for the disabled giant slalom."

2. Based on what Diana Golden said, you can predict that she

☐ a. will continue to face obstacles in her life with courage.

☐ b. will never ski again.

☐ c. will begin training so that she can compete in another sport.

3. Choose from the letters below to correctly complete the following statement. Write the letters on the lines.

On the positive side, _____ , but on the negative side _____ .

a. some people couldn't see past her disability

b. she had to retire before she won a medal as a nondisabled skier

c. Diana became a champion skier

4. Read paragraph 10. Then choose from the letters below to correctly complete the following statement. Write the letters on the lines.

According to paragraph 10, _____ because _____ .

a. she wanted to ski with regular ski poles

b. Diana had to learn a new way to balance herself

c. she wanted to ski at 65 miles per hour

5. What did you have to do to answer question 2?

☐ a. find an opinion (what someone thinks about something)

☐ b. find a description (how something looks)

☐ c. draw a conclusion (a sensible statement based on the text and your experience)

_____ Number of correct answers

Record your personal assessment of your work on the Critical Thinking Chart on page 74.

Personal Response

Describe a time when you had to overcome an obstacle or work hard to accomplish something that was important to you.

_____

_____

_____

_____

Self-Assessment

From reading this article, I have learned

_____

_____

_____

_____

CRITICAL THINKING

JACKIE ROBINSON
The Loneliest Season

Jackie Robinson and Brooklyn Dodgers president Branch Rickey look over Robinson's 1950 contract. The contract was for a sum between $30,000 and $35,000.

The meeting lasted three hours. Branch Rickey, general manager of the Brooklyn Dodgers, didn't want to take any chances. He wanted to make sure he had the right man for the job. The right man had to be willing to endure great public abuse. He had to be willing to "turn the other cheek." It was no task for a coward or a hothead. Rickey was looking for a black man to break into the whites-only world of major league baseball.

2 At that meeting on August 28, 1945, the baseball player being interviewed was Jackie Robinson. Jackie listened as Rickey explained why he wanted a black man on his team. Rickey was tired of seeing black talent go to waste. He knew that a man with Jackie's athletic ability could help the Dodgers. Jackie's superb talents might even lead the Dodgers to a pennant.

3 But being the first black man in the major leagues would not be easy. Rickey warned Jackie that there would be trouble. He gave Jackie a taste of the kind of name-calling that he would have to face. If Jackie couldn't take such insults from one man, what chance would he have against a crowd of 40,000 hostile baseball fans?

And it wouldn't be just the fans who would be hostile. Rickey pointed out that many of the white players would resent having a black man in the league.

4   It would be a dangerous situation. Jackie's presence could result in all kinds of violence. It could even lead to riots. Rickey knew that there was only one way it could work. If Jackie took the job, he would have to promise to avoid doing anything that would aggravate the already tense situation. He would have to remain silent in the face of vicious racial slurs and threats of violence. After telling Jackie all those things, Rickey paused and asked, "Well? Do you still want to go through with it?" Without hesitation, Jackie answered, "Yes. I am not afraid to try."

5   Who was this courageous man named Jackie Robinson? He was a man with great physical power, speed, and coordination. He was also a man of great moral character. The youngest of five children, Jackie was born in Cairo, Georgia, in 1919. Shortly after Jackie's birth, his father deserted the family. Jackie's mother moved her family to California in the hope that there would be more job opportunities there. She found work as a maid and fought hard to keep her family together. She did all she could to give her children a sense of self-worth and pride.

6   Despite his mother's support, life was not easy for Jackie. For a young black boy in the 1930s, California was not much better than rural Georgia. White children often called him "nigger." Many restaurants, playgrounds, and movie theaters were closed to him. Even the Pasadena municipal swimming pool was "for whites only."

7   Somehow Jackie survived the discrimination of those years without losing his dreams. He hoped to go to college and to become a baseball player. Jackie did manage to get into a junior college, and from there he made it to the University of California at Los Angeles (UCLA). At UCLA he ran track and joined the basketball and football teams. But baseball remained his real love.

8   When World War II broke out, Jackie joined the army and became a second lieutenant. Racial hatred followed him into the service. One day a bus driver ordered Jackie to move to the back of an army bus. The front, he said, was reserved for whites. Jackie became angry and refused to move. His refusal led to his arrest and trial in a military court. Although he was found innocent, he never forgot the insult. He told himself that he never wanted to be insulted like that again.

9   Then in August of 1945, he found himself sitting in Branch Rickey's office promising to endure even worse insults in silence. Jackie knew it would be difficult for him to control his temper. But like Rickey, Jackie knew that it was the only

Jackie Robinson is caught off first base in a game between the Boston Braves and the Brooklyn Dodgers, September 7, 1948.

way he could ever play major-league ball. So he decided to try.

10   After one highly successful year on the Dodgers' Triple-A farm team, Jackie was ready for the big time. So in the spring of 1947, Jackie Robinson put on a Dodger uniform for the first time. He was finally in the big leagues—big league baseball and big league racism. When the other members of the team heard of Jackie's arrival, several of them threatened to quit. Rickey talked to them, however, and got them to agree to try one season with Jackie in their midst. But they warned that if at the end of that time they were still unhappy they would either quit or would ask to be traded to another team.

11   When the official season opened in April, Jackie was a starting player for the Dodgers. But he had to play a position he had never played before. Jackie was an experienced second baseman. Unfortunately, the Dodgers already had a good man in that position. So Jackie was forced to play first base. When he took to the field on opening day, his mind was on how he would handle his new assignment. But his thoughts were soon interrupted by the booing and hissing of the crowd. He heard the fans jeering at him and calling him names. But just as he had promised Rickey, he did not react. He ignored the fans completely.

12   Gradually Jackie got used to the rude gestures and angry cries of the white fans. At every game, he had to put up with abuse from the stands. On top of that, he usually had to endure the hatred of the opposing team. When Jackie stepped up to bat, many pitchers threw the baseball directly at his head. When he was in the field, runners would try to step on his shoe, jabbing their spikes into his foot. Even Jackie's own teammates offered him little support.

13   As the season wore on, Jackie grew discouraged. It seemed he was making no progress. The fans continued to taunt him without mercy, and the players still did not accept him. Jackie began to wonder if it was worth all the pain and humiliation he was suffering. But something inside him would not let him give up. He continued to play and to endure. One sportswriter writing during that long summer of 1947 referred to Jackie as "the loneliest man I have ever seen in sports."

14   But lonely or not, Jackie Robinson's patience and persistence finally paid off. By the end of the season, he was triumphant. He batted .297, led the league in stolen bases, and was named Rookie of the Year. His daring baserunning and strong hitting also helped the Dodgers win their first pennant in six years. Jackie's superior athletic skill earned him the respect of his teammates and fellow athletes. By September, only one Dodger still wanted to be traded to another team, and most of the sports fans in America were on Jackie's side.

15   Jackie Robinson played 10 years in the major leagues and was elected to the National Baseball Hall of Fame after his retirement. Most importantly, he opened the door for other great black athletes. Baseball was eventually blessed by such legends as Willie Mays, Hank Aaron, and Reggie Jackson. While the talents of those men were tremendous, it was Jackie Robinson's willingness to suffer hatred and humiliation that made their careers possible. 🍃

If you have been timed while reading this article, enter your reading time below. Then turn to the Words-per-Minute Table on page 71 and look up your reading speed (words per minute). Enter your reading speed on the graph on page 72.

Reading Time: Lesson 3

_____ : _____
Minutes   Seconds

A | Finding the Main Idea

One statement below expresses the main idea of the article. One statement is too general, or too broad. The other statement explains only part of the article; it is too narrow. Label the statements using the following key:

M—Main Idea   **B—Too Broad**   **N—Too Narrow**

_____ 1. Jackie Robinson, a gifted black athlete, led the Brooklyn Dodgers to the pennant in 1947.

_____ 2. Jackie Robinson was a great baseball player who was discriminated against because he was black.

_____ 3. Jackie Robinson endured great personal abuse to become the first black baseball player in the major leagues.

_____ Score 15 points for a correct M answer.

_____ Score 5 points for each correct B or N answer.

_____ **Total Score:** Finding the Main Idea

B | Recalling Facts

How well do you remember the facts in the article? Put an X in the box next to the answer that correctly completes each statement about the article.

1. One of the reasons Branch Rickey asked Jackie Robinson to play for the Brooklyn Dodgers was that he
   - ☐ a. wanted to win the pennant.
   - ☐ b. thought Jackie would attract big crowds.
   - ☐ c. could pay Jackie less than the others.

2. Shortly after Jackie was born, his father
   - ☐ a. moved to California.
   - ☐ b. deserted the family.
   - ☐ c. died suddenly.

3. When Jackie Robinson joined the Dodgers in 1947,
   - ☐ a. some players threatened to quit.
   - ☐ b. Branch Rickey was fired.
   - ☐ c. he had just gotten out of the army.

4. During his first year with the Dodgers, Jackie Robinson played
   - ☐ a. first base.
   - ☐ b. second base.
   - ☐ c. third base.

5. Jackie Robinson played in the major leagues for
   - ☐ a. one year.
   - ☐ b. 10 years.
   - ☐ c. five years.

Score 5 points for each correct answer.

_____ **Total Score:** Recalling Facts

C | Making Inferences

When you combine your own experience and information from a text to draw a conclusion that is not directly stated in that text, you are making an inference. Below are five statements that may or may not be inferences based on information in the article. Label the statements using the following key:

C—Correct Inference   F—Faulty Inference

_____ 1. Branch Rickey thought that black athletes were much better than white athletes.

_____ 2. If Jackie Robinson had not been a top quality player on a top team, he would probably not have been accepted in the end.

_____ 3. During the 1930s and 1940s, discrimination against black Americans existed only in the southern United States.

_____ 4. Jackie Robinson had no hope that racial discrimination in the United States would someday disappear.

_____ 5. The black baseball players who followed Robinson into the majors did not have as difficult a time as he did.

Score 5 points for each correct answer.

_____ **Total Score:** Making Inferences

D | Using Words Precisely

Each numbered sentence below contains an underlined word or phrase from the article. Following the sentence are three definitions. One definition is closest to the meaning of the underlined word. One definition is opposite or nearly opposite. Label those two definitions using the following key. Do not label the remaining definition.

C—Closest   O—Opposite or Nearly Opposite

1. The right man had to be willing to endure great public <u>abuse</u>.

_____ a. mistreatment

_____ b. kindness

_____ c. complaints

2. Rickey pointed out that many of the white players would <u>resent</u> having a black man in the league.

_____ a. dislike

_____ b. be fearful of

_____ c. welcome

3. If Jackie took the job, he would have to promise to avoid doing anything that would <u>aggravate</u> the already tense situation.

_____ a. make worse

_____ b. interfere with

_____ c. improve

4. He would have to remain silent in the face of vicious racial <u>slurs</u> and threats of violence.

_____ a. insults

_____ b. stuttering

_____ c. polite remarks

5. The fans continued to <u>taunt</u> him without mercy, and the players still did not accept him.

_____ a. compliment

_____ b. challenge

_____ c. jeer at

_____ Score 3 points for each correct C answer.

_____ Score 2 points for each correct O answer.

_____ **Total Score:** Using Words Precisely

Enter the four total scores in the spaces below, and add them together to find your Reading Comprehension Score. Then record your score on the graph on page 73.

Score	Question Type	Lesson 3
_____	Finding the Main Idea	
_____	Recalling Facts	
_____	Making Inferences	
_____	Using Words Precisely	
_____	**Reading Comprehension Score**	

Author's Approach

Put an X in the box next to the correct answer.

1. What does the author mean by the statement "He had to be willing to 'turn the other cheek'"?

☐ a. Jackie Robinson could not look at the people who abused him.

☐ b. Jackie Robinson would be frequently hit in the face.

☐ c. Jackie Robinson could not react when people insulted him.

2. What is the author's purpose in writing "Jackie Robinson: The Loneliest Season"?

☐ a. To express an opinion about racism in the 1940s

☐ b. To inform the reader about Jackie's role in breaking baseball's color barrier

☐ c. To emphasize the similarities between black and white baseball players

3. What does the author imply by saying, "He told himself that he never wanted to be insulted like that again"?

☐ a. Jackie was a hothead.

☐ b. Jackie was proud.

☐ c. Jackie hated white people.

4. The author tells this story mainly by

☐ a. retelling Jackie's personal experiences as a baseball player.

☐ b. comparing the experiences of different athletes.

☐ c. telling different stories about breaking racial barriers.

_____ Number of correct answers

Record your personal assessment of your work on the Critical Thinking Chart on page 74.

Summarizing and Paraphrasing

Put an X in the box next to the correct answer for question 2. Follow the directions provided for the other question.

1. Look for the important ideas and events in paragraphs 11 and 12. Summarize those paragraphs in one or two sentences.

_____

_____

_____

_____

2. Choose the best one-sentence paraphrase for the following sentence from the article:

   "While the talents of those men were tremendous, it was Jackie Robinson's willingness to suffer hatred and humiliation that made their careers possible."

   ☐ a. Other black athletes would not have been willing to endure the hatred that Jackie Robinson experienced.

   ☐ b. Jackie Robinson's pioneering efforts paved the way for other black baseball players.

   ☐ c. The black baseball players who have followed Jackie Robinson have been better athletes.

   ┌───┐
   │ _____ Number of correct answers   │
   │   │
   │ Record your personal assessment of your work on the Critical │
   │ Thinking Chart on page 74.   │
   └───┘

Critical Thinking

Put an X in the box next to the correct answer for questions 1, 4, and 5. Follow the directions provided for the other questions.

1. Based on what the article said about the respect Jackie had earned by the end of his first season, you can predict that

   ☐ a. the black baseball players who followed him had an easier time.

   ☐ b. from then on, prejudice no longer existed in major league baseball.

   ☐ c. Jackie never suffered another racial insult on the field.

2. Choose from the letters below to correctly complete the following statement. Write the letters on the lines.

   On the positive side, _____ , but on the negative side _____.

   a. Jackie had to play first base

   b. Jackie had to play without the support of the fans or of his teammates

   c. Jackie broke into big league baseball

3. Read paragraph 8. Then choose from the letters below to correctly complete the following statement. Write the letters on the lines.

   According to paragraph 8, _____ happened because _____.

   a. he refused to move to the back of an army bus

   b. Jackie was found innocent

   c. Jackie's arrest and trial in a military court

4. If you were the manager of a baseball team, how could you use the information in the article to help a player ignore insults from fans?

☐ a. Like Branch Rickey, give the player a taste of the name-calling he would have to endure.

☐ b. Like Branch Rickey, allow the player to quit or be traded after one season.

☐ c. Like Branch Rickey, tell the player to turn the other cheek.

5. What did you have to do to answer question 1?

☐ a. draw a conclusion (a sensible statement based on the text and your experience)

☐ b. find an opinion (what someone thinks about something)

☐ c. find a fact (something that you can prove is true)

_____ Number of correct answers

Record your personal assessment of your work on the Critical Thinking Chart on page 74.

Personal Response

Would you recommend this article to other students? Explain.

_____

_____

_____

_____

Self-Assessment

I can't really understand how

_____

_____

_____

_____

GLADYS AYLWARD
Journey to Safety

The sun was just rising as Gladys Aylward prepared to set out across the wild and rugged mountains of China. She had to hurry. The Japanese soldiers were just a few hours from her village. Gladys was sorry to be leaving. For 10 years she had worked as a missionary in the remote hills of northern China. The people there had grown to like and trust her. But now, in 1940, China was at war with Japan. The Japanese were invading through northern China, and they were killing everyone they met along the way. Most Chinese civilians had already left the area.

2   As Gladys packed her few belongings, she tried not to think about the bullet wound in her back. Only 24 hours earlier, a Japanese soldier had spotted her in a field and had fired at her. One of his bullets had grazed her back. Although the wound was not serious, it caused her great pain.

3   She also tried not to think about how tired and hungry she was. Instead, she turned her attention to the children who were sleeping in every corner of the house. There were a hundred of them, all

Gladys Aylward led 100 children to safety over the rocky mountains of northern China. Her story served as the basis for the 1958 film The Inn of the Sixth Happiness *starring Ingrid Bergman.*

orphans. After their parents had been killed in the war, they had gone to Gladys for shelter. Most of them were very young—between four and eight years old. Only a handful were over 10. Gladys could not leave the children to be killed by the Japanese. She planned to take them all with her.

4   That would not be an easy thing to do. In fact, it would be almost impossible. They would have to walk over steep, rocky mountains that offered few trails. None of the children had good shoes. The small children could not walk far in a day. Even if they did get over the mountains, they would still have to cross the Yellow River, which was more than a mile wide. Only then could they get a train to Sian, a city where they would be safe.

5   Gladys knew that the journey would take several weeks. They would have to cover more than 250 difficult miles. She also knew that her food supply would not last more than three or four days. By herself, she could probably make it. But how far would she get with a hundred children? It didn't matter. Not for a moment did she consider leaving the children behind. She had to try to get them all safely to Sian. She had to try.

6   She quickly woke the children and helped them collect their belongings.

Every child carried his or her own blanket, bowl, and chopsticks. The small children were excited. To them it was a great adventure. As the group began walking, the little ones scrambled ahead over the rocks, laughing and shouting.

7   By noontime, however, they were hungry. They stopped by a mountain stream, and Gladys boiled some water in the iron pot she had brought along. Lunch was nothing more than boiled dough strings, but the children didn't mind. They had been eating the mush strands of dough all their lives. They ate so much, in fact, that Gladys got only a couple of spoonfuls. She did not complain, though, and from then on, two or three spoonfuls was her usual ration.

8   After lunch the children perked up. They walked several more miles before it got dark. As night fell, they came to the edge of a small village. Gladys found an old temple where the children could sleep. They were all so tired that they slept soundly. They did not notice the rats that swarmed over their bodies in the night.

9   The next few nights, the travelers were not lucky enough to find any villages. They had to sleep out among the rocks, with only their thin blankets to keep them warm. As the group struggled on, the children's spirits began to droop. By

then the children had holes in their shoes, and the bottoms of their feet were cut, blistered, and bleeding. They had used up their entire supply of food and were growing steadily weaker.

10   Gladys began carrying the blankets of the weakest ones. She also let the little ones take turns riding on her shoulders. Each day the scorching rays of the sun

Gladys Aylward shortly after her arrival in China.

beat down on them. They had no water, and they passed no rivers or streams. The children's skin became burned, and their lips cracked. On top of all that, they ran out of trails to follow. They had to scramble over huge boulders and down jagged cliffs.

11   Gladys tried hard to keep up the children's hopes. As they marched bravely along, she taught them hymns and told them stories. But by the seventh day she was worried. They had been without food for three days. She feared that if they did not find a village soon they would all die. Suddenly one of the older boys began shouting. "Soldiers!" he screamed. "Soldiers are coming!" Gladys felt panic rise within her. If the soldiers were Japanese, they would surely kill her and the children.

12   Luckily, the soldiers were Chinese. When Gladys told them of her plight, they reached into their knapsacks and pulled out enough food to feed Gladys and all the hungry children.

13   After the soldiers left, Gladys and the children moved on. For the next four days, they stumbled through the mountains. Many of the children were so tired and hungry that they cried constantly. Others had such sore feet that they could hobble only a hundred yards before stopping to rest. Gladys was getting weaker too, but she kept singing and talking and urging them on. She knew that their only hope was to keep going.

14   At last they reached a mountain peak from which they could see the Yellow River below. The children cheered as they hurried down toward the distant river. Along the way they came to a deserted village. Gladys sent the children out to scour the town for food. They found only some moldy grain, a few old dough cakes, and some vegetable scraps. Still, it was better than nothing. When they reached the river, Gladys threw all the food into her pot and boiled it up. Then she gave it to the children. Although she ate nothing, each child got a whole bowl full of food.

15   At that point the travelers faced a new problem. How were they going to get across the river? It was much too wide and deep to ford or swim, and there were no boats in the area. For the next three days they waited, helpless, by the water. Gladys prayed that a boat would pass by. On the third day, help finally arrived. A Chinese soldier found them and arranged to have a boat carry them all across the river. On the other side of the river was a village where the half-starved children were given a good meal. Then they boarded a train headed for Sian.

16   Their adventures, however, were not quite over. Part of the train tracks had been destroyed. So once again Gladys had to take the children into the mountains. Finally, they reached Sian. By that time Gladys was so weak that she could barely think straight. Still, she managed to get the children to an orphanage. There they

received food, clothing, and shelter. She had done it. By some miracle of determination and luck, she had led a hundred children safely across the mountains of China.

17   Shortly after the journey ended, Gladys Aylward collapsed and was taken to a hospital. Doctors discovered that she had been suffering from typhus for weeks. She had a temperature of 105 degrees and was developing pneumonia. For months the doctors didn't know if she would live. Eventually, though, she recovered and continued her missionary work. Although she later returned to her native England, Gladys Aylward never forgot the children she had saved during the war. And they never forgot her. They thought of her always as their mother. 🍃

If you have been timed while reading this article, enter your reading time below. Then turn to the Words-per-Minute Table on page 71 and look up your reading speed (words per minute). Enter your reading speed on the graph on page 72.

Reading Time: Lesson 4

_____ : _____
Minutes   Seconds

A | Finding the Main Idea

One statement below expresses the main idea of the article. One statement is too general, or too broad. The other statement explains only part of the article; it is too narrow. Label the statements using the following key:

M—Main Idea   **B—Too Broad**   **N—Too Narrow**

_____ 1. Gladys Aylward rescued a hundred homeless Chinese children by leading them on a difficult journey across the mountains of China.

_____ 2. Gladys Aylward was a missionary who spent many years helping the people of China.

_____ 3. Gladys kept the children's spirits up enough for them to keep walking, even when they were starving and in pain.

_____ Score 15 points for a correct M answer.

_____ Score 5 points for each correct B or N answer.

_____ **Total Score:** Finding the Main Idea

B | Recalling Facts

How well do you remember the facts in the article? Put an X in the box next to the answer that correctly completes each statement about the article.

1. Most of the children who struggled over the mountains were between
   - ☐ a. three and six years old.
   - ☐ b. four and eight years old.
   - ☐ c. 10 and 12 years old.

2. On the first night of the journey, Gladys and the children slept
   - ☐ a. out in the open among the rocks.
   - ☐ b. in an old temple.
   - ☐ c. in a deserted village.

3. Gladys tried to keep the children's spirits up by
   - ☐ a. singing songs and telling stories.
   - ☐ b. carrying the children's blankets, bowls, and chopsticks for them.
   - ☐ c. stopping to let the children swim in mountain streams.

4. One of the biggest problems Gladys and the children faced was
   - ☐ a. blinding snowstorms.
   - ☐ b. wild animals.
   - ☐ c. lack of food.

5. Upon reaching Sian, Gladys took the children to
   - ☐ a. their parents.
   - ☐ b. a temple.
   - ☐ c. an orphanage.

Score 5 points for each correct answer.

_____ **Total Score:** Recalling Facts

C Making Inferences

When you combine your own experience and information from a text to draw a conclusion that is not directly stated in that text, you are making an inference. Below are five statements that may or may not be inferences based on information in the article. Label the statements using the following key:

C—Correct Inference   F—Faulty Inference

_____ 1. Women and children were often killed in the war between China and Japan.

_____ 2. If the Japanese had not been invading northern China, Gladys would have stayed in her village.

_____ 3. Gladys Aylward's first concern was for her own safety.

_____ 4. All civilians leaving northern China during that time followed the same route that Gladys followed.

_____ 5. Gladys finally returned to England because she was driven out of China.

Score 5 points for each correct answer.

_____ **Total Score:** Making Inferences

D Using Words Precisely

Each numbered sentence below contains an underlined word or phrase from the article. Following the sentence are three definitions. One definition is closest to the meaning of the underlined word. One definition is opposite or nearly opposite. Label those two definitions using the following key. Do not label the remaining definition.

C—Closest   O—Opposite or Nearly Opposite

1. For 10 years she had worked as a missionary in the remote hills of northern China.

_____ a. steep

_____ b. close to large, highly populated cities

_____ c. wild and unsettled

2. One of his bullets had grazed her back.

_____ a. scraped

_____ b. broken

_____ c. traveled clean through

3. When Gladys told them of her plight, they reached into their knapsacks and pulled out enough food to feed Gladys and all the hungry children.

_____ a. bad situation

_____ b. missionary work

_____ c. good fortune

4. Others had such sore feet that they could <u>hobble</u> only a few hundred yards before stopping to rest.

_____ a. crawl

_____ b. walk freely

_____ c. limp painfully

5. Gladys sent the children out to <u>scour</u> the town for food.

_____ a. look quickly about

_____ b. scrub clean

_____ c. search thoroughly

_____ Score 3 points for each correct C answer.

_____ Score 2 points for each correct O answer.

_____ **Total Score:** Using Words Precisely

Enter the four total scores in the spaces below, and add them together to find your Reading Comprehension Score. Then record your score on the graph on page 73.

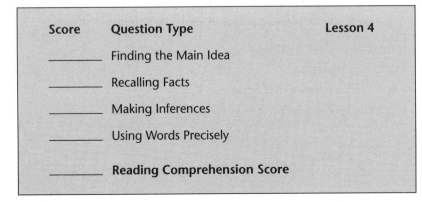

Score	Question Type	Lesson 4
_____	Finding the Main Idea	
_____	Recalling Facts	
_____	Making Inferences	
_____	Using Words Precisely	
_____	**Reading Comprehension Score**	

Author's Approach

Put an X in the box next to the correct answer.

1. What is the author's purpose in writing "Gladys Aylward: Journey to Safety"?

☐ a. To encourage the reader to act bravely

☐ b. To inform the reader about Gladys Aylward's bravery

☐ c. To entertain the reader with an adventure story

2. In this article, "the children's spirits began to droop" means the

☐ a. children's shoes were falling apart.

☐ b. children cried constantly.

☐ c. children were getting discouraged.

3. What does the author imply by saying that the children "thought of [Gladys Aylward] always as their mother"?

☐ a. The children no longer loved their own mothers.

☐ b. The children loved Gladys and were grateful to her.

☐ c. The children were too young to remember their own mothers.

4. How is the author's purpose for writing the article expressed in paragraph 14?

☐ a. The paragraph reveals the children's greed.

☐ b. The paragraph describes the difficulties of finding food on the journey.

☐ c. The paragraph shows that Gladys put the children's needs before her own.

_____ Number of correct answers

Record your personal assessment of your work on the Critical Thinking Chart on page 74.

CRITICAL THINKING

Summarizing and Paraphrasing

Put an X in the box next to the correct answer for questions 2 and 3. Follow the directions provided for the other question.

1. Complete the following one-sentence summary of the article using the lettered phrases from the phrase bank below. Write the letters on the lines.

> **Phrase Bank:**
> a. the hardships they experienced
> b. their safe arrival and the children's undying love for Gladys
> c. her determination to save the children

The article about Gladys Aylward's journey begins with _____, goes on to explain _____, and ends with _____.

2. Read the following statement about the article. Then read the paraphrase of that statement. Choose the reason that best tells why the paraphrase does not say the same thing as the statement.

Statement: Gladys Aylward led 100 orphaned Chinese children to safety during the war with Japan. Throughout the journey, Gladys put the needs of the children before her own. Her courage and selflessness inspired the children's love and respect.

Paraphrase: A woman rescued some children from the Japanese. The children thanked her for her efforts.

☐ a. Paraphrase says too much

☐ b. Paraphrase doesn't say enough.

☐ c. Paraphrase doesn't agree with the statement about the article.

3. Choose the best one-sentence paraphrase for the following sentence from the article:

"By then the children had holes in their shoes, and the bottoms of their feet were cut, blistered, and bleeding."

☐ a. The children took off their shoes and walked in their bare feet.

☐ b. The children did not have very good shoes.

☐ c. The children's shoes were torn, and their feet hurt terribly.

> _____ Number of correct answers
>
> Record your personal assessment of your work on the Critical Thinking Chart on page 74.

Critical Thinking

Put an X in the box next to the correct answer for questions 1, 3, and 4. Follow the directions provided for the other questions.

1. Based on Gladys Aylward's actions as told in this article, you can predict that she

☐ a. married and had many children of her own.

☐ b. continued to do good works in other parts of the world.

☐ c. adopted the orphaned children that she rescued.

2. Read paragraph 18. Then choose from the letters below to correctly complete the following statement. Write the letters on the lines.

According to paragraph 18, _____ because _____.

a. she had typhus

b. Gladys returned to England

c. Gladys collapsed

3. What effect did the destroyed train tracks on the route to Sian have on Gladys and the children?

☐ a.   They had to take a boat to the city.

☐ b.   They had to return to the mountains.

☐ c.   They had to wait beside the tracks for three days.

4. What did you have to do to answer question 1?

☐ a.   find an effect (something that happened)

☐ b.   find a contrast (how things are different)

☐ c.   draw a conclusion (a sensible statement based on the text and your experience)

5. In which paragraph did you find your information or details to answer question 3?

_____

_____ Number of correct answers

Record your personal assessment of your work on the Critical Thinking Chart on page 74.

Personal Response

What would you have done if the children had come to you for help?

_____

_____

_____

Self-Assessment

While reading the article, _____ was the easiest for me.

_____

_____

_____

_____

CRITICAL THINKING

CESAR CHAVEZ
Uniting Farm Workers

Cesar Chavez spent his entire childhood in poverty. He was born in 1927 in Arizona, where he lived until he was 11 years old. His parents, who were both Mexican, struggled to eke out a living by raising chickens, watermelons, and vegetables on their farm. Then in 1938, the Chavez family went broke. To survive, Cesar and his family became migrant workers, traveling from place to place, following the California crops. If there were walnuts to pick in southern California, that was where they went. When cherries were ready for harvesting in the north, they moved north. Although they worked hard, they did not earn much money. Growers refused to pay migrant workers fair wages. If a worker complained about the pay, the grower simply fired him or her. By 1939, there were 300,000 migrant workers in California, so growers could always find another person to do the job.

2 It didn't take Cesar Chavez long to discover how dismal the life of a migrant worker was. He spent countless days sweating in the hot California sun as he stooped to pick peas for less than a penny

Cesar Chavez traveled the country speaking at benefits to bring attention to the difficulties facing migrant farm workers in California.

a pound. He dug so many beets out of the wet Sacramento soil that the skin on his fingers cracked open. At night he and his family stayed in wretched cabins at the labor camps. They often had to share a bathroom with as many as 50 other families. One winter, when they had no money for rent, they were forced to live in a cold, wet tent.

3   Whenever Cesar wasn't working, he went to school. But even that was an unpleasant experience. The other children laughed at his Mexican accent. They made fun of him because he didn't have any shoes. They called him names and constantly threatened to beat him up. Because his family moved so often, he never stayed in one school long enough to make many friends. Between the ages of 11 and 15, he attended more than 30 different schools.

4   When Cesar was 21 years old, he married a woman named Helen. Four years later he got his first steady job. He became a staff member of the Community Service Organization, a group dedicated to protecting the civil rights of Mexican Americans. The group fought discrimination by encouraging Mexican Americans to register to vote.

5   Cesar worked for that organization until 1962. By then he and Helen had eight children. The family was not rich, but they had enough money to pay the bills. They also had a few hundred dollars in the bank.

6   Still, Cesar was not satisfied. He knew that the majority of Mexican Americans were not as lucky as he was. Most were still migrant farm workers with little hope for regular jobs or permanent homes. Cesar wanted desperately to help those farm workers. He felt that there was only one way they could improve their situation. All the workers had to join together. They had to form a union.

7   Cesar believed that he could organize such a union. But he knew it would not be easy. He would have to quit his job. His savings would soon be used up, and then he would be facing a return to the kind of poverty he had known as a child. He spent many nights talking it over with Helen. Finally, with her support, he took the big step. He resigned from his job and set out to organize a farm workers' union.

8   His plan was to win over the workers one at a time. To do that, he had to talk to them in person. For the next few weeks he traveled all over California. In just three months he covered almost 15,000 miles. He went out into the fields picking peas and staking grapes with workers, just to get a chance to talk to them. He invited many of them to his home to share his family's meager meals.

9   Each time he met with a worker, he explained that the union would fight for fair wages. It would demand better working conditions. It would do everything possible to protect the rights of farm workers. Cesar also told the workers that the union would never use violence to win its battles. He knew that in order to be successful the union would need public support. Because the public did not approve of violence, Cesar Chavez planned to use negotiations, strikes, and boycotts to fight the growers.

10   As word of Cesar's work spread, his dream of uniting farm workers became known as *La Causa*. That is a Spanish phrase that means "the cause." Before long, Cesar found other Mexican Americans who were willing to work for *La Causa* without pay. Just as the movement began to gain momentum, however, Cesar ran out of money. Unwilling to give up, he began to work part-time picking grapes. Helen also went to work as a farm laborer. The Chavez family scrimped on food, heat, and winter clothing in order to continue their work with *La Causa*.

Cesar Chavez used boycotts, strikes, and negotiations to improve working conditions for migrant farm workers.

11   On September 30, 1962, Cesar and his fellow workers officially founded the union. In 1965 the union, which became known as the United Farm Workers Association, still had just a few thousand members. Nonetheless, in the fall of that year Cesar took on a powerful enemy. For the next five years he and the union were locked in a battle with the grape growers of California.

12   The struggle began when the Filipino grape pickers decided to go on strike. The pickers were angry because the growers of table grapes had just lowered wages by more than 25 percent. The members of the United Farm Workers Association took a vote and decided to join the Filipinos. All the grape pickers in the union went on strike.

13   The growers were outraged, and tried every way that they could to break the strike. They sent guards out to harass the strikers. They beat striking workers and threatened to have Cesar Chavez killed. They even sprayed picket lines with pesticides.

14   But the workers believed strongly in what they were doing, and they did not give up. As Cesar had hoped, the public became upset by the violent tactics of the growers. Public opinion turned away from them. More and more people began to support the striking laborers. Cesar was pleased to see that, but he wanted to gain even more public support. So late in 1967, he decided to start a boycott of California grapes. He would ask the public to stop buying California grapes, as a show of support for the workers. He hoped the boycott would last until the growers agreed to negotiate with the union.

15   To start the boycott, Cesar sent 50 workers to New York City. The workers picketed stores where California grapes were sold. New Yorkers responded by supporting the boycott. The pickets then went to other cities and did the same thing. They found the people in those cities willing to help them too.

16   Although the boycott was successful, the grape growers still refused to accept the union. At that point, some union members grew impatient. They had been without work for over two years. They had families to support. They were desperate for food and money. In their frustration, they began to talk of violence. The only way to get the grape companies to listen, they said, was to kill a few growers.

17   Cesar tried to stop that kind of talk, but the workers wouldn't listen. Cesar worried that *La Causa* was losing sight of its goals. He felt that he had to find a way to make the union members stop and think. He decided to go on a fast. When the union members heard about it, they began visiting him to talk about the situation. As the farm workers rallied around him, they were reminded of the principles of *La Causa*. Soon all talk of violence ceased. Cesar himself grew weaker and weaker. The lack of food permanently damaged his health. But the fast worked. The spirit of the union members grew stronger. Finally, after 25 days, Cesar began to eat again. When he did, the union members were more determined and more united than ever before.

18   The struggle against the grape growers did not end there. It took two more years of strikes and boycotts before any real progress was made. But in 1970, the California grape growers gave in. They signed the first union contracts with farm workers. It had been a long and bitter battle. Ninety-five percent of the striking workers had been forced to sell their homes and their cars just to survive. And there were still many more battles to be fought. There were no union contracts yet for workers who picked lettuce, celery, broccoli, or strawberries.

19   Cesar Chavez knew all that, and he was determined to continue the battle. He decided to keep fighting until all crop growers treated their workers with fairness and respect. As he led his union into those new battles, he became a symbol for all oppressed workers. *La Causa* continued to gain support. And Cesar Chavez continued to stress the importance of unity and nonviolence in the struggle for justice. ◢

If you have been timed while reading this article, enter your reading time below. Then turn to the Words-per-Minute Table on page 71 and look up your reading speed (words per minute). Enter your reading speed on the graph on page 72.

Reading Time: Lesson 5

_____ : _____
Minutes   Seconds

A | Finding the Main Idea

One statement below expresses the main idea of the article. One statement is too general, or too broad. The other statement explains only part of the article; it is too narrow. Label the statements using the following key:

M—Main Idea   **B—Too Broad**   **N—Too Narrow**

_____ 1. Cesar Chavez worked for many years and made great personal sacrifices to form a union to protect the rights of farm workers.

_____ 2. Cesar Chavez was a Mexican American who cared a great deal about migrant farm workers.

_____ 3. Cesar Chavez helped win rights for California grape pickers by organizing a long and successful boycott of California table grapes.

_____ Score 15 points for a correct M answer.

_____ Score 5 points for each correct B or N answer.

_____ **Total Score:** Finding the Main Idea

B | Recalling Facts

How well do you remember the facts in the article? Put an X in the box next to the answer that correctly completes each statement about the article.

1. When Cesar Chavez quit his job, he
   - ☐ a. was living in a tent.
   - ☐ b. had a few thousand dollars in the bank.
   - ☐ c. was the father of eight children.

2. Because his family moved so often, Cesar
   - ☐ a. never went to school.
   - ☐ b. dropped out of school when he was 11 years old.
   - ☐ c. went to more than 30 different schools.

3. In an effort to break the grape pickers' strike, grape growers
   - ☐ a. brought in Filipino workers.
   - ☐ b. sprayed striking workers with pesticides.
   - ☐ c. raised wages 25 percent.

4. When union members heard of Cesar's fast, they
   - ☐ a. began to fast too.
   - ☐ b. went to visit him.
   - ☐ c. threatened to use violence to get him to eat again.

5. By the end of the strike against the grape growers,
   - ☐ a. several grape growers had been killed.
   - ☐ b. Cesar was ready to give up his leadership of the union.
   - ☐ c. most strikers had lost their homes.

Score 5 points for each correct answer.

_____ **Total Score:** Recalling Facts

C Making Inferences

When you combine your own experience and information from a text to draw a conclusion that is not directly stated in that text, you are making an inference. Below are five statements that may or may not be inferences based on information in the article. Label the statements using the following key:

C—Correct Inference   F—Faulty Inference

_____ 1. Cesar Chavez loved being a migrant worker.

_____ 2. Cesar Chavez didn't care if his children grew up in poverty.

_____ 3. Before the boycott, many Americans were not aware of the working conditions of migrant farm laborers.

_____ 4. If Cesar Chavez had not fasted, the farm workers would have begun to use violence.

_____ 5. The only crop that Filipinos picked was grapes.

Score 5 points for each correct answer.

_____ **Total Score:** Making Inferences

D Using Words Precisely

Each numbered sentence below contains an underlined word or phrase from the article. Following the sentence are three definitions. One definition is closest to the meaning of the underlined word. One definition is opposite or nearly opposite. Label those two definitions using the following key. Do not label the remaining definition.

C—Closest   O—Opposite or Nearly Opposite

1. He became a staff member of the Community Service Organization, a group dedicated to protecting the civil rights of Mexican Americans.

    _____ a. uninterested

    _____ b. related to

    _____ c. devoted

2. At night he and his family stayed in wretched cabins at the labor camps.

    _____ a. miserable

    _____ b. expensive

    _____ c. delightful

3. As word of Cesar's work spread, his dream of uniting farm workers became known as *La Causa*.

    _____ a. dividing

    _____ b. fighting for

    _____ c. bringing together

4. They sent guards out to <u>harass</u> the strikers.

_____ a. beat up

_____ b. help greatly

_____ c. bother repeatedly

5. As the farm workers rallied around him, they were reminded of the <u>principles</u> of *La Causa*.

_____ a. heads of educational institutions

_____ b. guiding beliefs

_____ c. lawlessness

_____ Score 3 points for each correct C answer.

_____ Score 2 points for each correct O answer.

_____ **Total Score:** Using Words Precisely

Enter the four total scores in the spaces below, and add them together to find your Reading Comprehension Score. Then record your score on the graph on page 73.

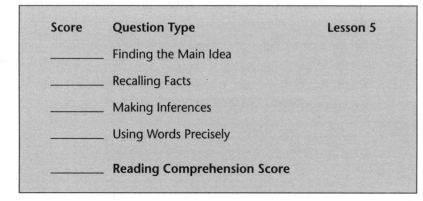

Score	Question Type	Lesson 5
_____	Finding the Main Idea	
_____	Recalling Facts	
_____	Making Inferences	
_____	Using Words Precisely	
_____	**Reading Comprehension Score**	

Author's Approach

Put an X in the box next to the correct answer.

1. The author uses the first sentence of the article to

☐ a. inform the reader about the conditions of Cesar's youth.

☐ b. describe the experience of growing up poor in California.

☐ c. compare picking walnuts with picking cherries.

2. From the statements below, choose those that you believe the author would agree with.

☐ a. Cesar Chavez was an impatient man.

☐ b. Cesar Chavez did not believe in violence as a way to achieve change.

☐ c. Cesar was willing to sacrifice his health for *La Causa*.

3. Based on the statement from the article, "The Chavez family scrimped on food, heat, and winter clothing in order to continue their work with *La Causa*," you can conclude that the author wants the reader to think that Cesar's family

☐ a. ruined their health for the union.

☐ b. supported his union.

☐ c. resented the union.

4. Choose the statement below that is the weakest argument for joining Cesar's farm workers' union.

☐ a. Joining the union will help prevent growers from firing workers when they complain.

☐ b. Joining the union will help improve working conditions in the fields.

☐ c. Joining the union will allow members to make new friends.

_____ Number of correct answers

Record your personal assessment of your work on the Critical Thinking Chart on page 74.

Summarizing and Paraphrasing

Put an X in the box next to the correct answer for question 2. Follow the directions provided for the other question.

1. Reread paragraph 17 in the article. Below, write a summary of the paragraph in no more than 25 words.

_____

_____

_____

_____

Reread your summary and decide whether it covers important parts of the paragraph. Next, decide how to shorten the summary to 15 words or less without leaving out any essential information. Write this summary below.

_____

_____

_____

2. Choose the statement that correctly restates the following sentence from the article:

"Because the public did not approve of violence, Cesar Chavez planned to use negotiations, strikes, and boycotts to fight the growers."

☐ a. The public did not agree with Cesar Chavez's plan to use violence against the growers.

☐ b. Even though the public was not on his side, Cesar Chavez knew he would have to fight the growers.

☐ c. In order to gain public support, Cesar Chavez wanted to use only nonviolent methods against the growers.

_____ Number of correct answers

Record your personal assessment of your work on the Critical Thinking Chart on page 74.

Critical Thinking

Put an X in the box next to the correct answer for questions 1 and 2. Follow the directions provided for the other questions.

1. Which of the following statements from the article is an opinion rather than a fact?

☐ a. "The only way to get the grape companies to listen, they said, was to kill a few growers."

☐ b. "But the workers believed strongly in what they were doing, and they did not give up."

☐ c. "The members of the United Farm Workers Association took a vote and decided to join the Filipinos."

CRITICAL THINKING

2. Based on the events in the article, you can predict that the following will happen next:

☐ a. Cesar would use violence to make crop growers treat their workers with respect.

☐ b. Cesar would fight to gain union contracts for other farm workers.

☐ c. Cesar would fast until the growers of lettuce, celery, broccoli, and strawberries agreed to sign union contracts.

3. Choose from the letters below to correctly complete the following statement. Write the letters on the lines.

In the article, _____ and _____ are different.

a. the United Farm Workers Association

b. *La Causa*

c. the Community Service Organization

4. Choose from the letters below to correctly complete the following statement. Write the letters on the lines.

According to the article, the grape boycott caused _____ to _____, and the effect was _____.

a. the first union contract with farm workers

b. the public

c. stop buying grapes

5. Which paragraphs from the article provide evidence that supports your answer to question 4?

_____

_____ Number of correct answers

Record your personal assessment of your work on the Critical Thinking Chart on page 74.

Personal Response

What was most surprising or interesting to you about this article?

_____

_____

_____

_____

Self-Assessment

The part I found most difficult about the article was

_____

_____

_____

_____

I found this difficult because

_____

_____

_____

_____

CRITICAL THINKING

MIEP GIES
A Dangerous Secret

Miep Gies didn't look like a criminal. To a casual observer, she appeared meek and obedient. But every day for two years, Miep Gies broke the law. Today, the world salutes her for having the courage and compassion to do that.

2   In 1939, Miep (pronounced MEEP) was living and working in Amsterdam, Netherlands. She worked for a company that sold jam-making products. That fall, World War II broke out. A few months later, Hitler and his Nazi soldiers took over the Netherlands. Miep knew Hitler hated all Jews. Still, it was shocking to see Nazi soldiers begin to round up Jews and ship them off to forced labor camps. Miep Gies was not a Jew, but she hated what was happening. Rage smoldered inside her every time she saw a Nazi uniform.

3   By 1942, Miep's own boss was in danger. His name was Otto Frank. Mr. Frank desperately wanted to protect his wife Edith and their two daughters, Margot and Anne. But what could he do? As a Jew, he had no rights. He and his family weren't allowed to leave Amsterdam. They weren't allowed even to ride the local streetcars or own a

Miep Gies holds a new edition of The Diary of Anne Frank, *which includes passages that were omitted from the original edition.*

bicycle. They had to wear big yellow stars on their coats so Nazi soldiers could spot them easily. And any day now, the soldiers would come and take them all away.

4   Miep knew that some Jews tried to avoid capture. Many ran for the coast, hoping to get onto a ship bound for England. Others snuck out to the countryside, hiding in abandoned shops or old barns. Miep wondered if the Franks had ever thought of fleeing. But she kept her questions to herself. She was sure Mr. Frank would do what he thought best.

5   Then one day, Otto Frank called Miep into his office.

6   "Miep," he said, "I have a secret to confide in you."

7   Miep listened as Otto explained his plan. There were some unfinished rooms in the attic above his office. He wanted to hide his family there. Would Miep be willing to help him?

8   It was a lot to ask. In order to help the Franks, Miep would somehow have to smuggle food into the attic every day. What if someone saw her? Besides, how would she get the food in the first place? Wartime rationing meant that people could buy only enough to feed their own families. If Miep started buying food for four extra people, surely someone would notice. The neighbors would become suspicious and report her to the authorities.

9   Furthermore, it was not just four people who would be hiding in the attic. Mr. Frank had invited a business partner to come with him, as well as the man's wife and son. So Miep would really need to take care of seven people.

10   Miep knew all this. She knew that if the Nazis found out, they would probably send her to a labor camp, too. Yet when Otto Frank turned to her, Miep never hesitated. Would she help? "Of course," she said quickly.

11   Mr. Frank hoped to prepare the attic rooms before they moved in. He wanted to bring in clothing and arrange the beds. But there wasn't time. In early July, Margot Frank received a notice in the mail telling her she had been assigned to a labor camp. She was supposed to report right away. When Otto Frank heard that, he immediately contacted Miep. Early the next morning, they made their move. Miep brought Margot to the secret attic rooms. The rest of the group followed a short time later.

12   And so began 25 months of hiding. The two families in the attic suffered in many ways. Their secret rooms were hot in the summer, cold in the winter. During the day, when the building was filled with office workers, they had to be very quiet. When sickness struck, they simply had to wait it out. There was no way they could get medical attention. Anne's eyes began to bother her, and she suffered from bad headaches. Her parents knew she needed glasses, but they couldn't risk sending her out to an eye doctor. Although all seven people worked together as best they could, their nerves grew jagged. At times, tension filled the air.

13   Miep, meanwhile, had problems of her own. Every morning she went to work early. She had to get to the office before the regular workers arrived. Quickly she slipped up to the attic, where her friends gave her a list of the food they needed. Then later each day, Miep went shopping. She tried to appear casual when she walked into a store and ordered large quantities of food.

14   After a while, Miep began to trust one particular grocer. He never asked questions, but filled her orders as best he

The building in Amsterdam where Anne Frank and her family hid for over two years.

could. Miep believed he understood—and approved of—what she was doing. But one day when she entered his shop, the grocer wasn't there. In his place was his terror-stricken wife.

15   "What's the matter?" asked Miep.

16   "My husband's been arrested," the woman whispered frantically. "They've taken him away. He was hiding Jews. Two Jews. I don't know what they'll do to him."

17   Miep's heart raced. She felt a wave of fear for this gentle man who had been so good to her. She knew it could just as easily have been she who had been discovered. In addition, she knew that now it would be harder than ever to get food for the people in the attic.

18   Luckily, Miep found another grocer who was willing to sell her extra food. Still, it was getting more and more difficult to find anything decent. The Nazis were diverting food supplies away from Amsterdam to feed their own troops. Sometimes Miep spent hours shopping and still wound up with half-rotten vegetables and spoiled meat.

19   The months dragged by. Miep struggled to keep up the spirits of those in the attic. She brought them news of the war—especially when the news was encouraging. She smuggled in armloads of books for them to read. She brought writing paper so young Anne could keep a diary. She managed to find sweets for the children. Once Miep and her husband even spent the night in the attic to help relieve their friends' boredom and unhappiness.

20   Miep's life became even more stressful when she and her husband agreed to hide a Jewish boy in their own apartment. Miep also took pity on her dentist, a Jewish man named Fritz Pfeffer. She got the Franks' permission to bring him to the attic to live.

21   By the summer of 1944, Miep had reason to hope that the war would soon end. Hitler's troops were retreating from several European positions. But the war did not end soon enough for the Frank family. Miep had been exceedingly careful. She had done all she could to protect the Franks and the others in the attic. She had tried never to draw attention to herself or her activities. Still, someone figured out what was going on and turned her in. Records show that the Nazis received an anonymous phone call telling them about the Jews in the attic.

22   On August 4, Nazis raided Miep's office building. They went directly to the secret rooms. The next thing Miep knew, her eight friends were being marched away by Nazi police. It was the last time she ever saw most of them.

23   Miep herself was lucky. She was not arrested. After the Nazis took away her friends, she hurried to the attic. There, lying on the floor, she spotted Anne's diary. She picked it up and hid it in her desk drawer. It was a dangerous thing to keep, for it showed how deeply involved Miep had been in the conspiracy to save the Franks. But Miep didn't care. She promised herself she would keep the diary safe until Anne returned.

24   Tragically, Anne Frank did not return. She and the others were sent to concentration camps. Although Otto Frank survived the ordeal, none of the others made it out alive. Miep was shattered when she learned the news.

25   After the war, Miep gave Anne's diary to Otto. In time, he decided to publish it. That way, he hoped, others could learn how vibrant and kind-hearted his young daughter had been.

26   Many years later, Miep herself wrote a book, which she called *Anne Frank Remembered*. In it she wrote, "I am not a hero…. I was only willing to do what was asked of me and what seemed necessary at the time." But on this point, the rest of the world disagrees. To people who know the story, Miep Gies is a hero. She is a woman of remarkable courage and conviction. She will always be remembered as a beacon of goodness and light during some of history's darkest days.

If you have been timed while reading this article, enter your reading time below. Then turn to the Words-per-Minute Table on page 71 and look up your reading speed (words per minute). Enter your reading speed on the graph on page 72.

Reading Time: **Lesson 6**

_____ : _____

Minutes   Seconds

A | Finding the Main Idea

One statement below expresses the main idea of the article. One statement is too general, or too broad. The other statement explains only part of the article; it is too narrow. Label the statements using the following key:

M—Main Idea   **B—Too Broad**   **N—Too Narrow**

_____ 1. Every day Miep Gies shopped for food for the friends she was hiding in the secret rooms.

_____ 2. Miep Gies hated the Nazis and did everything she could to oppose them.

_____ 3. Risking her own life, Miep Gies hid the Frank family and other Jews from the Nazis for more than two years.

_____ Score 15 points for a correct M answer.

_____ Score 5 points for each correct B or N answer.

_____ **Total Score:** Finding the Main Idea

B | Recalling Facts

How well do you remember the facts in the article? Put an X in the box next to the answer that correctly completes each statement about the article.

1. Miep agreed to hide the Franks in
   ☐ a. her own apartment.
   ☐ b. the attic above Mr. Frank's office.
   ☐ c. an abandoned barn in the countryside.

2. The first person to move into the rooms was
   ☐ a. Otto Frank.
   ☐ b. Anne Frank.
   ☐ c. Margot Frank.

3. During the day, the families in the secret rooms had to be quiet because
   ☐ a. the building was filled with office workers.
   ☐ b. the building was too hot in the summer.
   ☐ c. Anne Frank suffered from bad headaches.

4. The grocer Miep trusted
   ☐ a. made an anonymous call to the Nazi police.
   ☐ b. sold her half-rotten vegetables and spoiled meats.
   ☐ c. was arrested for hiding Jews.

5. After the Nazis took Miep's friends away,
   ☐ a. the Nazis arrested Miep.
   ☐ b. Miep found Anne's diary.
   ☐ c. Miep published Anne's diary.

Score 5 points for each correct answer.

_____ **Total Score:** Recalling Facts

C | Making Inferences

When you combine your own experience and information from a text to draw a conclusion that is not directly stated in that text, you are making an inference. Below are five statements that may or may not be inferences based on information in the article. Label the statements using the following key:

C—Correct Inference   F—Faulty Inference

_____   1. The grocer approved of Miep's actions because he, too, was hiding Jews.

_____   2. Everyone in Amsterdam was helping the Jews hide from the Nazis.

_____   3. The people living in the secret rooms always got along very well.

_____   4. Miep Gies is a modest, hard-working woman.

_____   5. The Nazis discovered the hiding place because Miep had been careless.

Score 5 points for each correct answer.

_____ **Total Score:** Making Inferences

D | Using Words Precisely

Each numbered sentence below contains an underlined word or phrase from the article. Following the sentence are three definitions. One definition is closest to the meaning of the underlined word. One definition is opposite or nearly opposite. Label those two definitions using the following key. Do not label the remaining definition.

C—Closest   O—Opposite or Nearly Opposite

1. Rage <u>smoldered</u> inside her every time she saw a Nazi uniform.

_____   a. cooled down

_____   b. turned to ashes

_____   c. burned slowly

2. At times, <u>tension</u> filled the air.

_____   a. thick fog

_____   b. a relaxed atmosphere

_____   c. anxiety

3. "My husband's been arrested," the woman whispered <u>frantically</u>.

_____   a. with great fear

_____   b. calmly

_____   c. very softly

4. Although Otto Frank survived the <u>ordeal</u>, none of the others made it out alive.

_____   a. experiment

_____   b. agreeable experience

_____   c. terrible nightmare

5. She is a woman of remarkable courage and <u>conviction</u>.

_____ a. strong beliefs

_____ b. curiosity

_____ c. faithlessness

_____ Score 3 points for each correct C answer.

_____ Score 2 points for each correct O answer.

_____ **Total Score:** Using Words Precisely

Enter the four total scores in the spaces below, and add them together to find your Reading Comprehension Score. Then record your score on the graph on page 73.

Score	Question Type	Lesson 6
_____	Finding the Main Idea	
_____	Recalling Facts	
_____	Making Inferences	
_____	Using Words Precisely	
_____	**Reading Comprehension Score**	

Author's Approach

Put an X in the box next to the correct answer.

1. The main purpose of the first paragraph is to

☐ a. describe Miep's appearance.

☐ b. inform readers about Miep's courage.

☐ c. convey a mood of fear.

2. Which of the following statements from the article best describes Miep Gies?

☐ a. "She appeared meek and obedient."

☐ b. "She had tried to never draw attention to herself or her activities."

☐ c. "She is a woman of remarkable courage and conviction."

3. In this article, "Miep's heart raced" means Miep

☐ a. had a heart condition.

☐ b. was very frightened.

☐ c. had been running too fast.

4. What does the author imply by saying "She will always be remembered as a beacon of goodness and light during some of history's darkest days"?

☐ a. Miep showed great bravery and caring at a time when Nazi cruelty and hatred controlled much of Europe.

☐ b. Miep will always be remembered for bringing Anne Frank's diary to light.

☐ c. Miep was good because she hid the Franks and other Jews from the Nazis.

_____ Number of correct answers

Record your personal assessment of your work on the Critical Thinking Chart on page 74.

Summarizing and Paraphrasing

Put an X in the box next to the correct answer for questions 2 and 3. Follow the directions provided for the other question.

1. Complete the following one-sentence summary of the article using the lettered phrases from the phrase bank below. Write the letters on the lines.

> **Phrase Bank:**
> a. her willingness to hide the Jewish families
> b. the arrest of Miep's friends
> c. how she managed to take care of them

   The article about Miep Gies begins with _____, goes on to explain _____, and ends with _____.

2. Read the following statement about the article. Then read the paraphrase of that statement. Choose the reason that best tells why the paraphrase does not say the same thing as the statement.

   Statement: Although the person who telephoned the Nazis remained anonymous, he or she must have been watching Miep's movements.

   Paraphrase: Miep knew who made the phone call to the Nazis.

   ☐ a. Paraphrase says too much.

   ☐ b. Paraphrase doesn't say enough.

   ☐ c. Paraphrase doesn't agree with the statement about the article.

3. Choose the best one-sentence paraphrase for the following sentence from the article:

   "Although all seven people worked together as best they could, their nerves grew jagged."

   ☐ a. Tensions arose in spite of the people's efforts to get along.

   ☐ b. The people living in the attic always felt nervous.

   ☐ c. The people living in the attic had a lot of work to do.

> _____ Number of correct answers
>
> Record your personal assessment of your work on the Critical Thinking Chart on page 74.

Critical Thinking

Put an X in the box next to the correct answer for questions 1 and 4. Follow the directions provided for the other questions.

1. From the article, you can predict that if the Nazis had not raided the secret attic

   ☐ a. Anne Frank and the others would have survived the war.

   ☐ b. Miep would have considered herself a hero.

   ☐ c. Anne Frank's diary would never have been published.

2. Using what you know about Miep Gies and what the article tells about her grocer, name three ways Miep is similar to and three ways Miep is different from the grocer. Cite the paragraph number(s) where you found details in the article to support your conclusions.

   Similarities

   _____

   _____

   _____

Differences

_____

_____

_____

3. Choose from the letters below to correctly complete the following statement. Write the letters on the lines.

   According to the article, an anonymous phone call caused _____ to _____, and the effect was _____].

   a. raid the secret attic

   b. all but one of those taken away died

   c. the Nazi police

4. What did you have to do to answer question 2?

   ☐ a. find a contrast (how things are different)

   ☐ b. find a description (how something looks)

   ☐ c. find a comparison (how things are the same)

   _____ Number of correct answers

   Record your personal assessment of your work on the Critical Thinking Chart on page 74.

Personal Response

A question I would like answered by Miep Gies is "_____?"

_____

_____

_____

_____

Self-Assessment

Before reading this article, I already knew

_____

_____

_____

_____

MAHATMA GANDHI
The Peaceful Way

Mahatma Gandhi led nonviolent protests against British rule to help India win its independence from the British Empire in 1947.

To most people, salt is just something to sprinkle on popcorn. But to the people of India, salt is something special. It is a symbol of their struggle for independence from Britain. It is a symbol of the Salt March of 1930, which was a turning point in that struggle. And it is a symbol of Mahatma Gandhi, the man who led the Salt March.

2   Gandhi believed that India should be a free country. He did not like seeing his people ruled by foreigners. The Salt March was his way of protesting one aspect of British rule. The British had passed a law making it illegal for the people of India to collect their own salt. Everyone was required to buy salt from the British. In early 1930, Gandhi believed it was time to break that law. He decided to walk to the sea to gather his own salt "from the ocean created by God."

3   It was not the first time that Gandhi had decided to break the law. He had been leading protests against British rule for years. Many of the protests had been illegal, and Gandhi had often been jailed. But he didn't mind. He believed that if a

law was morally wrong it was his duty to break it. That was part of his philosophy, which he called Satyagraha (suh-TYAH-gruh-huh). The philosophy called for the use of moral force to change the wrongs of society. A person who used Satyagraha did not hate his enemies. He did not ever use violence against them. But neither did he give in. According to Satyagraha, a person should act in a way that was morally right and sooner or later the forces of right would win out. A person practicing Satyagraha would not follow ways that he or she believed to be wrong.

4   In March of 1930, Gandhi wrote to the British viceroy, or governor, stating his intention to lead a salt march. The viceroy did not reply. So on March 12, Gandhi and 75 followers set out on the march. Gandhi was 61 years old. On the march, Gandhi wore only a simple loincloth. In his right hand he carried a thick bamboo staff to lean on as he walked. Day after day, the hot sun beat down on him and his followers. Still they kept walking, averaging 10 miles a day. As they walked, they were joined by hundreds of other Indians. Every step of the way, people poured out of their huts to greet Gandhi and join in the march. The revered leader stopped frequently to speak to the people. He reminded them of their duty to love

one another and to resist the British through nonviolent means. Gandhi told his followers, "I would rather die a dog's death and have my bones licked by dogs than that I should return home a broken man."

5   Throughout the march, Gandhi watched for the arrival of the viceroy's soldiers. He fully expected to be arrested. He had even named a substitute to take over leadership of the march after his arrest. But days passed and no soldiers showed up. The viceroy had decided not to make an arrest, because he thought the march would simply peter out and die. He was wrong.

6   The Salt March soon became world news. People from many different countries followed Gandhi's every move. They marveled at the thin old man who was capturing the love and admiration of the Indian people. Every day, Gandhi was offered a ride in a cart. But he always refused. He insisted on walking all the way. He knew the world was watching and waiting.

7   Finally, on April 5, Gandhi reached the coast. By that time almost 10,000 people were marching with him. Gandhi was feeling weak. He had walked 241 miles. The trip had tired him. But he was also very happy, and when a reporter asked

him what he wanted from the march, he said, "I want world sympathy in this battle of Right against Might."

8   All that night Gandhi and his followers prayed by the water's edge. Early the next morning, Gandhi held a religious ceremony and bathed briefly in the sea to

Gandhi with his wife Katsurba on their return to India, 1915.

purify himself. Then, at 8:30 A.M., he stopped by the water's edge to pick up a handful of salt. Thousands of Indians shouted their joy. For the first time in their lives, all the people who had marched with Gandhi felt truly free.

9   After picking up the salt, Gandhi was sure he would be arrested immediately. But he was not. It was another three weeks before the British put him in jail. In the meantime, the news of his defiance spread all across India. The word *salt* was on everyone's lips. Almost overnight, it came to mean independence for India. The people were in an uproar. Many of them followed Gandhi's example by going down to the sea and gathering salt for themselves. They also began burning British cloth in the streets and holding public demonstrations against Britain.

10   On April 27, Gandhi was finally arrested for his role in the Salt March. As he was taken to jail, he calmly began singing his favorite hymn. He was not upset or worried. His faith in Satyagraha remained unshaken. He was certain that sooner or later Britain would have to give up its unjust position as ruler of India.

11   In the end, Britain did grant India the right of self-government. But that did not happen quickly. India's fight for independence had only begun with the Salt March. It took another 17 years for the country to win its freedom. During those 17 years, Gandhi was arrested again and again. Some of his followers were beaten and even killed. But Gandhi never abandoned his belief in nonviolent protest. And with Gandhi as their leader, neither did the people of India. 🍃

If you have been timed while reading this article, enter your reading time below. Then turn to the Words-per-Minute Table on page 71 and look up your reading speed (words per minute). Enter your reading speed on the graph on page 72.

Reading Time: **Lesson 7**

_____ : _____

Minutes   Seconds

A | Finding the Main Idea

One statement below expresses the main idea of the article. One statement is too general, or too broad. The other statement explains only part of the article; it is too narrow. Label the statements using the following key:

M—Main Idea   **B—Too Broad**   **N—Too Narrow**

_____ 1. Mahatma Gandhi was a much-loved and respected moral leader of the Indian people.

_____ 2. Gandhi led the people of India in a nonviolent struggle for independence, beginning with a march to the sea to collect salt, in defiance of British law.

_____ 3. In 1930, Mahatma Gandhi led thousands of Indian people on an illegal march to the sea to collect salt.

_____ Score 15 points for a correct M answer.

_____ Score 5 points for each correct B or N answer.

_____ **Total Score:** Finding the Main Idea

B | Recalling Facts

How well do you remember the facts in the article? Put an X in the box next to the answer that correctly completes each statement about the article.

1. Under British rule, it was illegal for Indians to
   ☐ a. gather salt.
   ☐ b. buy salt.
   ☐ c. use salt.

2. A person living according to the philosophy of Satyagraha uses
   ☐ a. physical force.
   ☐ b. illegal force.
   ☐ c. moral force.

3. Immediately after receiving Gandhi's letter in March of 1930, the viceroy
   ☐ a. called out his troops.
   ☐ b. put Gandhi in jail.
   ☐ c. did nothing.

4. The first thing Gandhi did when he reached the coast was
   ☐ a. pray with his followers.
   ☐ b. pick up a handful of salt.
   ☐ c. bathe briefly in the sea to purify himself.

5. Three weeks after the Salt March,
   ☐ a. India was granted independence.
   ☐ b. Gandhi was arrested.
   ☐ c. the people of India revolted against the British.

Score 5 points for each correct answer.

_____ **Total Score:** Recalling Facts

C Making Inferences

When you combine your own experience and information from a text to draw a conclusion that is not directly stated in that text, you are making an inference. Below are five statements that may or may not be inferences based on information in the article. Label the statements using the following key:

C—Correct Inference   **F—Faulty Inference**

_____ 1. The British did not view Satyagraha the way that Gandhi did.

_____ 2. The people of India needed salt more than the people of other countries did.

_____ 3. Gandhi felt it was important to the cause that he personally walk all the way to the sea.

_____ 4. Gandhi was pleased when the reports of his Salt March appeared in newspapers around the world.

_____ 5. The salt law was not the only British law that upset Gandhi and the Indian people.

Score 5 points for each correct answer.

_____ **Total Score:** Making Inferences

D Using Words Precisely

Each numbered sentence below contains an underlined word or phrase from the article. Following the sentence are three definitions. One definition is closest to the meaning of the underlined word. One definition is opposite or nearly opposite. Label those two definitions using the following key. Do not label the remaining definition.

C—Closest   **O—Opposite or Nearly Opposite**

1. The viceroy had decided not to make an arrest, because he thought that the march would simply <u>peter out</u>.

_____ a. gather strength

_____ b. slowly die out

_____ c. change direction

2. They <u>marveled at</u> the thin old man who was capturing the love and admiration of the Indian people.

_____ a. were filled with wonder by

_____ b. were bored by

_____ c. were angry with

3. But he was also very happy, and when a reporter asked him what he wanted from the march, he said, "I want world <u>sympathy</u> in this battle of Right against Might."

_____ a. peace

_____ b. opposition

_____ c. support

4. In the meantime, the news of his <u>defiance</u> spread all across India

_____ a. open rebellion

_____ b. obedience

_____ c. nonviolence

5. His faith in Satyagraha remained <u>unshaken</u>.

_____ a. weak

_____ b. confused

_____ c. firm

_____ Score 3 points for each correct C answer.

_____ Score 2 points for each correct O answer.

_____ **Total Score:** Using Words Precisely

Enter the four total scores in the spaces below, and add them together to find your Reading Comprehension Score. Then record your score on the graph on page 73.

Score	Question Type	Lesson 7
_____	Finding the Main Idea	
_____	Recalling Facts	
_____	Making Inferences	
_____	Using Words Precisely	
_____	**Reading Comprehension Score**	

Author's Approach

Put an X in the box next to the correct answer.

1. What is the author's purpose in writing "Mahatma Gandhi: The Peaceful Way"?

☐ a. To express an opinion about the British rulers of India

☐ b. To inform the reader about Gandhi's nonviolent struggle for India's independence

☐ c. To convey a mood about the Salt March

2. Which of the following statements from the article best describes Mahatma Gandhi?

☐ a. "Gandhi was 61 years old."

☐ b. "He had been leading protests against British rule for years."

☐ c. "But Gandhi never abandoned his belief in nonviolent protest."

3. In this article, "'I want world sympathy in this battle of Right against Might'" means Gandhi wanted

☐ a. people to feel sorry for him and for the Indian people.

☐ b. to gain world-wide support for the Salt March.

☐ c. to gain world-wide support for the cause of Indian independence.

3. Choose the statement below that best describes the author's position in paragraph 5.

☐ a. Gandhi was a beloved leader whose conviction inspired others.

☐ b. Gandhi needed the help of his followers to continue his march.

☐ c. Gandhi hated the British and hoped that they would test his determination.

_____ Number of correct answers

Record your personal assessment of your work on the Critical Thinking Chart on page 74.

Summarizing and Paraphrasing

Put an X in the box next to the correct answer for question 3. Follow the directions provided for the other questions.

1. Look for the important ideas and events in paragraphs 9 and 10. Summarize those paragraphs in one or two sentences.

_____

_____

_____

2. Complete the following one-sentence summary of the article using the lettered phrases from the phrase bank below. Write the letters on the lines.

Phrase Bank:

a. Gandhi's philosophy

b. Gandhi's continuing fight for India's independence

c. the events of the Salt March

The article about Mahatma Gandhi begins with _____, goes on to explain _____, and ends with _____.

3. Read the following statement about the article. Then read the paraphrase of that statement. Choose the reason that best tells why the paraphrase does not say the same thing as the statement.

Statement: Gandhi believed that opposing unjust laws was morally right.

Paraphrase: According to Gandhi, the Indian people were justified in collecting their own salt because the law forbidding this practice was unfair.

☐ a. Paraphrase says too much.

☐ b. Paraphrase doesn't say enough.

☐ c. Paraphrase doesn't agree with the statement about the article.

_____ Number of correct answers

Record your personal assessment of your work on the Critical Thinking Chart on page 74.

Critical Thinking

Put an X in the box next to the correct answer for questions 1 and 3. Follow the directions provided for the other questions.

1. From the article, you can predict that if a British soldier beat Mahatma Gandhi,

☐ a. Gandhi's followers would physically attack the soldier.

☐ b. Gandhi would not try to hurt the soldier.

☐ c. Gandhi would defend himself by striking back.

2. Think about cause–effect relationships in the article. Fill in the blanks in the cause–effect chart, drawing from the letters below.

Cause   Effect

_____   Gandhi led the Salt March.

Gandhi gathered some salt.   _____

Gandhi continued to break British laws.   _____

a.   Gandhi was arrested again and again.

b.   The British made it illegal for the Indian people to collect their own salt.

c.   Many of the Indian people began to protest British rule.

3. Of the following theme categories, which would this article fit into?

☐ a.   love conquers all

☐ b.   good triumphs over evil

☐ c.   right makes might

4. Which paragraphs from the article provide evidence that supports your answer to question 2?

_____

_____ Number of correct answers

Record your personal assessment of your work on the Critical Thinking Chart on page 74.

Personal Response

Why do you think Mahatma Gandhi insisted on walking all the way to the sea during the Salt March?

_____

_____

_____

_____

Self-Assessment

One good question about this article that was not asked would be

_____

_____

_____

and the answer is

_____

_____

_____

CRITICAL THINKING

Compare and Contrast

Think about the articles you have read in Unit One. Pick the four heroes you most enjoyed reading about or were most inspired by. Write their names in the first column of the chart below. Use information you learned from the articles to fill in the empty boxes in the chart.

My Hero	Where did this person live and work?	What heroic thing did he or she do?	What made these actions unusual?

The person I admire most is _____ because _____

_____

Words-per-Minute Table

Unit One

Directions: If you were timed while reading an article, refer to the Reading Time you recorded in the box at the end of the article. Use this words-per-minute table to determine your reading speed for that article. Then plot your reading speed on the graph on page 72.

Lesson / No. of Words	Sample / 860	1 / 1104	2 / 1006	3 / 1254	4 / 1334	5 / 1532	6 / 1473	7 / 974	Seconds
1:30	573	736	671	836	889	1021	982	649	90
1:40	516	662	604	752	800	919	884	584	100
1:50	469	602	549	684	728	836	803	531	110
2:00	430	552	503	627	667	766	737	487	120
2:10	397	510	464	579	616	707	680	450	130
2:20	369	473	431	537	572	657	631	417	140
2:30	344	442	402	502	534	613	589	390	150
2:40	323	414	377	470	500	575	552	365	160
2:50	304	390	355	443	471	541	520	344	170
3:00	287	368	335	418	445	511	491	325	180
3:10	272	349	318	396	421	484	465	308	190
3:20	258	331	302	376	400	460	442	292	200
3:30	246	315	287	358	381	438	421	278	210
3:40	235	301	274	342	364	418	402	266	220
3:50	224	288	262	327	348	400	384	254	230
4:00	215	276	252	314	334	383	368	244	240
4:10	206	265	241	301	320	368	354	234	250
4:20	198	255	232	289	308	354	340	225	260
4:30	191	245	224	279	296	340	327	216	270
4:40	184	237	216	269	286	328	316	209	280
4:50	178	228	208	259	276	317	305	202	290
5:00	172	221	201	251	267	306	295	195	300
5:10	166	214	195	243	258	297	285	189	310
5:20	161	207	189	235	250	287	276	183	320
5:30	156	201	183	228	243	279	268	177	330
5:40	152	195	178	221	235	270	260	172	340
5:50	147	189	172	215	229	263	253	167	350
6:00	143	184	168	209	222	255	246	162	360
6:10	139	179	163	203	216	248	239	158	370
6:20	136	174	159	198	211	242	233	154	380
6:30	132	170	155	193	205	236	227	150	390
6:40	129	166	151	188	200	230	221	146	400
6:50	126	162	147	184	195	224	216	143	410
7:00	123	158	144	179	191	219	210	139	420
7:10	120	154	140	175	186	214	206	136	430
7:20	117	151	137	171	182	209	201	133	440
7:30	115	147	134	167	178	204	196	130	450
7:40	112	144	131	164	174	200	192	127	460
7:50	110	141	128	160	170	196	188	124	470
8:00	108	138	126	157	167	192	184	122	480

Minutes and Seconds

Seconds

Plotting Your Progress: Reading Speed

Unit One

Directions: If you were timed while reading an article, write your words-per-minute rate for that in the box under the number of the lesson. Then plot your reading speed on the graph by putting a small X on the line directly above the number of the lesson, across from the number of words per minute you read. As you mark your speed for each lesson, graph your progress by drawing a line to connect the X's.

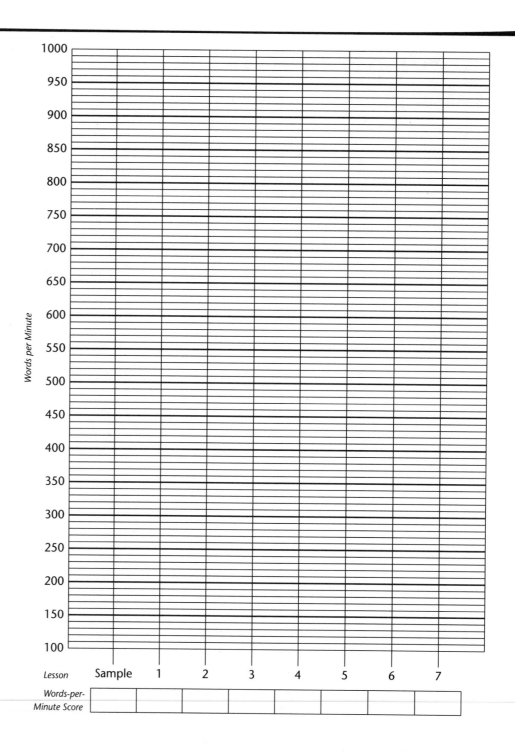

Lesson	Sample	1	2	3	4	5	6	7
Words-per-Minute Score								

Plotting Your Progress: Reading Comprehension

Unit One

Directions: Write your Reading Comprehension score for each lesson in the box under the number of the lesson. Then plot your score on the graph by putting a small X on the line directly above the number of the lesson and across from the score you earned. As you mark your score for each lesson, graph your progress by drawing a line to connect the X's.

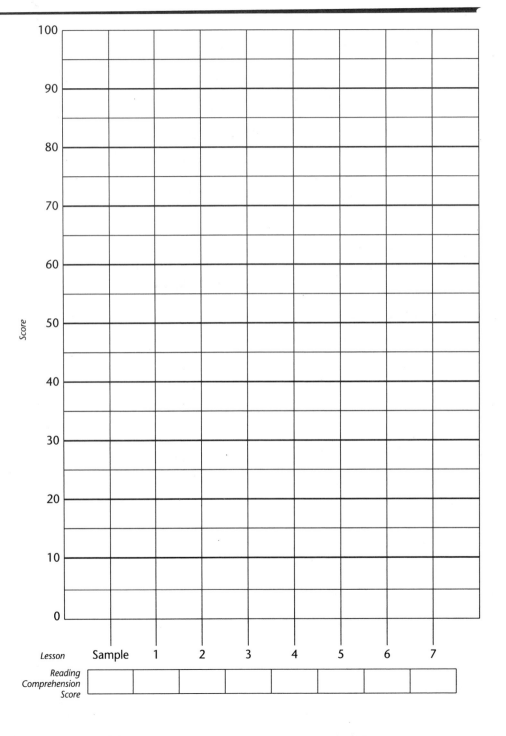

Lesson	Sample	1	2	3	4	5	6	7
Reading Comprehension Score								

Plotting Your Progress: Critical Thinking

Unit One

Directions: Work with your teacher to evaluate your responses to the Critical Thinking questions for each lesson. Then fill in the appropriate spaces in the chart below. For each lesson and each type of Critical Thinking question, do the following: Mark a minus sign (–) in the box to indicate areas in which you feel you could improve. Mark a plus sign (+) to indicate areas in which you feel you did well. Mark a minus-slash-plus sign (–/+) to indicate areas in which you had mixed success. Then write any comments you have about your performance, including ideas for improvement.

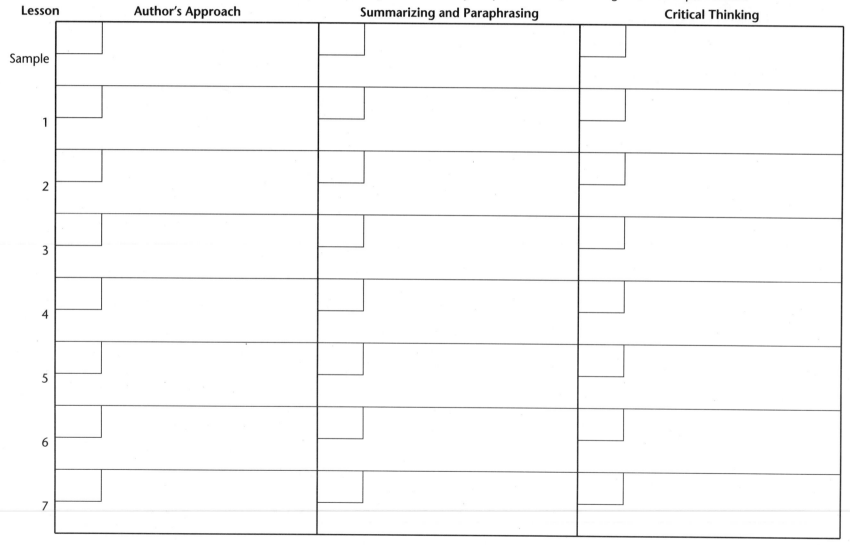

Lesson	Author's Approach		Summarizing and Paraphrasing		Critical Thinking	
Sample						
1						
2						
3						
4						
5						
6						
7						

UNIT TWO

MATTHEW HENSON
To the Top of the World

It took Commander Robert E. Peary 18 years and nine separate attempts to reach the North Pole. Each attempt required a superhuman effort. No one had ever reached the North Pole. Many men had tried, but all had failed. Some had even lost their lives trying to cross the difficult terrain from Greenland to the very top of the world. On each expedition, Peary faced starvation, blinding sun, and endless Arctic winters. Most people today think of Commander Peary as a hero. Indeed, his actions did show tremendous bravery. But what most people don't know is that there is a second hero in this story. He accompanied Peary on every journey to the North. He saved Peary's life on several occasions and made his ultimate success possible. The man's name was Matthew Henson.

2   Matt Henson was a black man born in Charles County, Maryland, in 1867. By the time he was 12 years old, both his parents had died and Henson had gone to work as a cabin boy on a merchant ship. He never had a chance to go to school, but the captain of the ship taught him to

Matthew Henson (at far left in photo) and four Eskimos halt for lunch on their way to the North Pole in 1909.

read and write. When the captain died in 1884, Henson became a stockboy in a hat store. He longed for adventure, but as a black man in a prejudiced white society, there was little chance that he would ever have the opportunity to join in any great undertaking.

3 In 1887, however, Henson had the good fortune of meeting a man named Robert Peary. Peary was looking for a servant to accompany him on an exploration of Nicaragua. Henson leaped at the chance to go along. Peary and Henson worked well together. In the jungles of Central America, they became less like master and servant and more like comrades.

4 On returning to the United States, Peary announced his plan to try to conquer the North Pole. He could not make the journey alone, of course, and although he was impressed with Henson's work, he didn't think Henson would want to head out to the frigid north. "After all," Peary said, "you're a black man. You work well in warm, sunny climates. But you would find it very difficult to be up north."

5 Peary probably did not mean this as an insult. He was merely reflecting the ignorance of the times. But to Matthew Henson, the words were a direct challenge. His response was, "I'll go north with you, sir, and I think I'll stand it as well as any man."

6 Henson's words turned out to be an understatement. To survive in the bitter and barren land of northern Greenland, it was necessary to adopt the lifestyle of the Eskimos. From the beginning, it was Henson who showed the most promise of learning Eskimo ways. This was partly because the Eskimos helped him more than they helped Peary. They spent countless hours teaching him their language and customs. They helped him because they trusted him. Although he was a foreigner, he had dark skin like theirs, so they assumed he was an Eskimo from a foreign land. Also, they liked his kindness, cheerfulness, and willingness to learn. Soon the Eskimos not only trusted Henson but loved him, as well.

7 From the Eskimos, Henson learned to make clothing from animal skins and to build and repair sleds using local tools. Most importantly, he mastered the use of the Eskimo dogsled. Driving a dogsled involved managing a group of 10 or more half-wild dogs. The driver had to be able to crack a 28-foot whip in the air just inches above a dog's head. Henson mastered that difficult skill in just one month.

8 On their first trip to the Arctic, in 1891, Peary, Henson, and the other members of the expedition discovered why no earlier explorers had ever reached the North Pole. The Pole was hundreds of miles beyond the northernmost Eskimo settlement in Greenland. To get past that settlement, Peary's group had to travel in the winter, when the ice around the Pole was thick enough to support the weight of men and dogs. But the winter weather in that part of the world was almost beyond

Matthew Henson, who was instrumental in helping Robert E. Peary reach the North Pole in 1909

human endurance. The temperature often fell to 50 or 60 degrees below zero. The wind whipped across the ice with bone-chilling fury. Violent snowstorms arose without warning. Some sled dogs became sick and died; others went mad and had to be shot. The game animals that lived in the region began migrating southward, so the group faced the possibility of starvation. And throughout the winter, the men were plagued by frostbite.

9   Given such bleak conditions, it is not surprising that the expedition did not reach the Pole. In fact, on that trip Peary only got to within 500 miles of the North Pole. For the next 17 years, however, he kept trying. Each time, he faced the same dangers. And each time, he had to recruit a new crew. Few people cared to spend more than one winter in the frozen Arctic wasteland of northern Greenland. Only Matt Henson stuck with Peary on every trip for the entire 18 years.

10   With every journey to the North, Peary became more and more dependent on Henson. Henson even saved Peary's life several times. On one such occasion, the two men went out on the ice alone to scout a new area. While crossing an ice bridge between two cliffs, Peary stepped on a weak spot. The ice gave way and he fell through up to his armpits. He hung trapped with only his head and shoulders still visible. If he made one false move, he would fall to his death hundreds of feet below. It was Henson's calm response that saved him. Henson quickly grabbed a

rope, dropped to his stomach, and crawled out onto the thin ice. As Peary clung to the ice around him, Henson managed to tie a rope around his chest. Then, for 15 tense minutes, Henson inched his way back, pulling Peary out of the hole to safety.

11   On another occasion, Henson saved Peary from a charging musk-ox. Peary had fallen to his knees and was watching helplessly as the ox ran toward him. The beast was only a few feet from Peary when Henson grabbed his gun and fired off a shot, killing the ox. On still another trip, Peary developed a severe case of frostbite in his toes. Henson tried to warm the toes by holding them against his own stomach, but that didn't help. Henson then carried Peary back to their ship. The ship's doctor had to cut off the toes to keep gangrene from setting in.

12   In 1909, on their ninth and final journey to the North, Peary and Henson finally reached their goal. With four Eskimos and about 40 dogs, they made it all the way to the North Pole. By that time, Peary was exhausted. Years of struggling against the Arctic climate had weakened him. Henson was tired too, but he had reserves of energy that astonished even Peary.

13   After taking some photographs and resting for a few hours, the men began the long journey home. Peary lasted only an hour before collapsing. Tears streamed down his face. Like Henson, he had permanent burns and blisters on his eyes

from the intense glare of the Arctic sun. But he seemed to have suddenly become almost totally blind. He looked and acted like a tired old man. In a role that had become familiar, Matt Henson rescued Peary. He loaded him onto a sled and, in just 16 days, dragged him the 400 miles back to their camp.

14   In finally reaching the North Pole, Robert Peary became a famous man. He was made an admiral in the Navy, and he retired to a life of ease. For Matt Henson, however, there was no fame, no public recognition. Because he was a black man, no one was interested in his story. Matthew Henson lived the rest of his life in a small apartment in Harlem, a black community in New York City. For a while he worked as a handyman in a garage. Later he became a messenger in the United States Customs House. 🍂

If you have been timed while reading this article, enter your reading time below. Then turn to the Words-per-Minute Table on page 133 and look up your reading speed (words per minute). Enter your reading speed on the graph on page 134.

Reading Time: **Lesson 8**

_____ : _____
Minutes   Seconds

A | Finding the Main Idea

One statement below expresses the main idea of the article. One statement is too general, or too broad. The other statement explains only part of the article; it is too narrow. Label the statements using the following key:

M—Main Idea　　　**B—Too Broad**　　　**N—Too Narrow**

_____　1. Matthew Henson, a courageous and loyal black man, made it possible for Robert Peary to be credited as the first man to reach the North Pole.

_____　2. Matthew Henson saved Robert Peary's life a number of times on various expeditions to the North Pole.

_____　3. Matthew Henson was a brave black man who did not get recognition for his part in Robert Peary's expeditions to the North Pole.

_____　Score 15 points for a correct M answer.

_____　Score 5 points for each correct B or N answer.

_____　**Total Score:** Finding the Main Idea

B | Recalling Facts

How well do you remember the facts in the article? Put an X in the box next to the answer that correctly completes each statement about the article.

1. The first place Peary and Henson went together was
   - ☐ a. Africa.
   - ☐ b. Greenland.
   - ☐ c. Nicaragua.

2. When Peary met him, Matthew Henson was working as a
   - ☐ a. cabin boy.
   - ☐ b. stockboy.
   - ☐ c. servant.

3. One of the reasons the Eskimos liked Henson was that he was
   - ☐ a. a foreigner.
   - ☐ b. dark skinned.
   - ☐ c. an Eskimo.

4. Peary and Henson finally reached the North Pole on their
   - ☐ a. fifth attempt.
   - ☐ b. seventh attempt.
   - ☐ c. ninth attempt.

5. The Navy honored Peary by
   - ☐ a. making him an admiral.
   - ☐ b. giving him a medal.
   - ☐ c. retiring him.

Score 5 points for each correct answer.

_____　**Total Score:** Recalling Facts

C | Making Inferences

When you combine your own experience and information from a text to draw a conclusion that is not directly stated in that text, you are making an inference. Below are five statements that may or may not be inferences based on information in the article. Label the statements using the following key:

C—Correct Inference   **F—Faulty Inference**

_____ 1. It was not possible to reach the North Pole during the summer months.

_____ 2. The Eskimos knew more about how to survive in the Arctic than anyone else did.

_____ 3. No matter how well the men dressed, when they were in the far North they were always in danger of getting frostbite.

_____ 4. After the first expedition to the North Pole, Henson continued to accompany Peary only out of loyalty to him.

_____ 5. Matthew Henson was honored when he was given the job as a messenger in the United States Customs House.

Score 5 points for each correct answer.

_____ **Total Score:** Making Inferences

D | Using Words Precisely

Each numbered sentence below contains an underlined word or phrase from the article. Following the sentence are three definitions. One definition is closest to the meaning of the underlined word. One definition is opposite or nearly opposite. Label those two definitions using the following key. Do not label the remaining definition.

C—Closest   O—Opposite or Nearly Opposite

1. He longed for adventure, but as a black man in a <u>prejudiced</u> white society, there was little chance that he would ever have the opportunity to join in any great undertaking.

_____ a. treating certain people unfairly on the basis of an unfounded negative opinion

_____ b. segregated

_____ c. fair minded in making judgments

2. In the jungles of Central America, they became less like master and servant and more like <u>comrades</u>.

_____ a. enemies

_____ b. close companions

_____ c. communists

3. He was merely reflecting the <u>ignorance</u> of the times.

_____ a. fashion

_____ b. learning

_____ c. lack of knowledge

4. To survive in the bitter and barren land of northern Greenland, it was necessary to <u>adopt</u> the lifestyle of the Eskimos.

_____ a. change

_____ b. take on

_____ c. give up

5. Henson was tired too, but he had reserves of energy that <u>astonished</u> even Peary.

_____ a. frightened

_____ b. amazed

_____ c. did not impress

_____ Score 3 points for each correct C answer.

_____ Score 2 points for each correct O answer.

_____ **Total Score:** Using Words Precisely

Enter the four total scores in the spaces below, and add them together to find your Reading Comprehension Score. Then record your score on the graph on page 135.

Score	Question Type	Lesson 8
_____	Finding the Main Idea	
_____	Recalling Facts	
_____	Making Inferences	
_____	Using Words Precisely	
_____	**Reading Comprehension Score**	

Author's Approach

Put an X in the box next to the correct answer.

1. The main purpose of the first paragraph is to

☐ a. entertain readers with an adventure story.

☐ b. introduce Matthew Henson and describe his role in the early North Pole expeditions.

☐ c. express an opinion about racial prejudice.

2. From the statements below, choose those that you believe the author would agree with.

☐ a. Robert Peary did not deserve to receive all of the credit for reaching the North Pole successfully.

☐ b. Peary could have reached the North Pole without Matthew Henson's help.

☐ c. The world should learn about Matthew Henson's contribution to the North Pole expeditions.

3. Based on the statement from the article, "Because he was a black man, no one was interested in his story," you can conclude that the author wants the reader to think that

☐ a. Henson was bitter over his lack of recognition.

☐ b. Henson did not get the recognition he deserved.

☐ c. people didn't believe that Henson had played an important role in the expeditions.

CRITICAL THINKING

4. Choose the statement below that best describes the author's position in paragraph 3.

☐ a. Peary was prejudiced against black people.

☐ b. Peary was an ignorant man.

☐ c. Peary accepted many of the 19th-century preconceptions about black people.

_____ Number of correct answers

Record your personal assessment of your work on the Critical Thinking Chart on page 136.

Summarizing and Paraphrasing

Put an X in the box next to the correct answer.

1. Below are summaries of the article. Choose the summary that says all the most important things about the article but in the fewest words.

☐ a. Although Matthew Henson, a black man, helped make Robert Peary's expedition to the North Pole a success, his contributions were not acknowledged.

☐ b. Matthew Henson accompanied Robert Peary to the North Pole.

☐ c. Matthew Henson, a black man, repeatedly saved Robert Peary's life and accompanied him on every journey to the North Pole. Henson, however, did not receive the acclaim he deserved.

2. Choose the sentence that correctly restates the following sentence from the article:

"He longed for adventure, but as a black man in a prejudiced white society, there was little chance that he would ever have the opportunity to join in any great undertaking."

☐ a. Because he was black, Henson endured a great deal of discrimination from white society.

☐ b. Because he was black, Henson was not allowed to take part in adventures that included white people.

☐ c. Because he was black, Henson would probably never have the chance to take part in an important enterprise.

_____ Number of correct answers

Record your personal assessment of your work on the Critical Thinking Chart on page 136.

Critical Thinking

Put an X in the box next to the correct answer for questions 2, 3, and 4. Follow the directions provided for the other questions.

1. For each statement below, write O if it expresses an opinion and write F if it expresses a fact.

_____ a. Robert Peary would never have reached the North Pole without Matthew Henson.

_____ b. Matthew Henson deserved to become famous for his role in the North Pole expeditions.

_____ c. Peary believed that Henson would have trouble adjusting to conditions in the North Pole.

2. From the article, you can predict that if Henson had been a white man, he

   ☐ a. wouldn't have accompanied Peary to the North Pole.

   ☐ b. would have become as famous as Robert Peary.

   ☐ c. would not have saved Peary's life over and over again.

3. What was the cause of Peary's having to have his toes cut off?

   ☐ a. He developed a severe case of frostbite.

   ☐ b. He developed gangrene.

   ☐ c. He was attacked by a musk-ox.

4. What did you have to do to answer question 1?

   ☐ a. find an opinion (what someone thinks about something)

   ☐ b. find a cause (why something happened)

   ☐ c. find a fact (something that you can prove is true)

5. In which paragraph did you find your information or details to answer question 3?

   _____

   ┌───┐
   │ _____ Number of correct answers   │
   │   │
   │ Record your personal assessment of your work on the Critical │
   │ Thinking Chart on page 136.   │
   └───┘

Personal Response

I know how Matthew Henson feels because

_____

_____

_____

_____

Self-Assessment

While reading the article, _____ was the easiest for me to understand.

_____

_____

_____

_____

CRITICAL THINKING

MARINA SILVA
Saving Amazonia's Rain Forests

arina Silva de Souza grew up deep in the rain forests of Brazil. From a young age, she knew her way along jungle paths, over streams, and through misty swamps. For her, the forests were not just some exotic tourist spot. They were home. Only later, after Marina grew up, did she realize her home was in danger. Unless someone did something to save the Brazilian rain forests, they would soon be ruined forever.

2   Marina was born in 1958 in a remote part of Brazil called Amazonia. In this region, the mighty Amazon River flows through jungles so dense you need a knife to cut your way through them. Marina's family was like all the others who lived in the region. Her father was a *seringueiro*, someone who made his living collecting rubber from rubber trees. Like other seringueiros, he didn't earn much money. He barely made enough to keep his family alive. As a child, Marina knew the sharp pangs of hunger. She sometimes went without food for 24 hours at a time.

3   When the family did eat, their meals often consisted of rodents and other

Before and After: A Venezuelan rain forest (left) and the burning of a Brazilian rain forest (right)

creatures that roamed the jungles. Marina herself began hunting and fishing at an early age, trying to bring in a little extra food for her family. Marina's parents had 11 children, three of whom died as babies. As the oldest surviving child, Marina helped care for her sisters and brother. Also, she often went out into the forest and helped her father tap rubber trees.

4   When Marina was 15, her mother died. Now Marina had to take on even more duties. She had never been to school. She didn't know how to read or write. But suddenly she had to help figure out the weight of the rubber her family collected. Otherwise, the men who bought the rubber would try to cheat them.

5   Quickly Marina mastered enough arithmetic to protect the family business. That experience made her hungry for more knowledge. But she had little hope of ever getting a formal education. That was beyond the reach of most seringueiras.

6   The following year, Marina Silva came down with hepatitis, a liver disease. She grew weak. Soon she could no longer go out and do the strenuous work involved in tapping rubber trees. Where others saw sickness, however, Marina saw opportunity. She told her father it might

be best if she left the rain forest. She asked if she could move to the city, where she could get an easier job—and where she could go to school.

7   Her father agreed, and so at age 16, Marina found herself alone in a big city. She worked as a maid by day and attended

Marina Silva de Souza holds the Goldman Environmental Award.

classes at night. Going to school was a dream come true. Marina quickly learned to read and write. She absorbed everything in the books she read. In three short years, she flew through all the work of elementary school, junior high, and high school. By age 20, she had earned a college degree in history.

8   Student life opened Marina's eyes to many things. Some of the things she learned did not come out of a book. For one thing, she began to get a bigger, clearer picture of what was happening to Amazonia's rain forests. She learned that cattle ranchers were moving deeper into the rain forests every day. The ranchers were cutting down the forests and destroying the land. Miners and loggers were also invading the rain forests. Soon, Marina realized, the place where she grew up would be a wasteland.

9   Marina decided to fight the ranchers. She heard about another seringueiro who was doing the same thing. His name was Chico Mendes. By the early 1980s, Marina had joined forces with Chico. She devoted herself to protecting what was left of Brazil's great rain forests. She wanted to save not just the trees, but also families like her own, who had tapped rubber trees in the jungle for generations.

10   With Chico, Marina set up *empates*. These were peaceful demonstrations held in the rain forests. Rubber tappers gathered where new roads were being built. They blocked ranchers who tried to enter the area. Marina, Chico, and other rubber tappers boldly stood their ground in the face of huge trucks, bulldozers, and other equipment. The ranchers, furious at the obstruction, tried to get the people to move. But the rubber tappers held their ground.

11   Day after day, Marina put her life in danger to lead empates. She and Chico set up dozens of roadblocks. In the process, they organized rubber tappers into an independent trade union.

12   News of the empates spread fast. World opinion backed the rubber tappers. Pressure was placed on the Brazilian government to protect the rain forests and keep out the ranchers. Then, on December 22, 1988, the movement was dealt a cruel blow. A rancher named Darcy Alves murdered Chico Mendes.

13   It was not the first time a rancher had used violence on the seringueiros. And it would not be the last. Over a 20-year span starting in the mid-1970s, ranchers made plans to kill 1,600 protesters. One person they hoped to kill was Marina Silva. She knew she was in danger, but she refused to back down. Instead, she pushed harder than ever to finish what she and Chico Mendes had started.

14   "When they killed Chico, they thought they would kill the movement," Marina said. She promised that would not happen. Thanks to her courage and dedication, the empates continued. And at last, Marina got the government to help the rubber tappers. It set aside more than 4 million acres of Amazonia as reserves. The reserves would be managed by the rubber tappers themselves. That meant the seringueiros could continue to live and work in the rain forest as they always had.

15   Marina was pleased, but she felt her job was not done. Her people still needed many things. They needed more schools and better health care. In 1994, Marina Silva ran for a seat on the Brazilian Federal Senate. Many thought she would lose. No seringueira had ever been elected to the Senate. But Marina surprised them; she won the election.

16   As a political leader, Marina became a powerful voice for the rights of her people and for the protection of the rain forests. In 1996, She won the prestigious Goldman Environmental Award. The award named her a "hero of the earth." By then, her people had another name for her. They called her simply the "Amazon legend."

If you have been timed while reading this article, enter your reading time below. Then turn to the Words-per-Minute Table on page 133 and look up your reading speed (words per minute). Enter your reading speed on the graph on page 134.

Reading Time: Lesson 9

_____ : _____
Minutes   Seconds

A Finding the Main Idea

One statement below expresses the main idea of the article. One statement is too general, or too broad. The other statement explains only part of the article; it is too narrow. Label the statements using the following key:

M—Main Idea   **B—Too Broad**   **N—Too Narrow**

_____ 1. Marina Silva won an award that named her a "hero of the earth."

_____ 2. Marina Silva became a powerful voice for the rights of the Brazilian people.

_____ 3. Marina Silva successfully fought to protect the rain forests and the rights of rubber tappers who lived and worked in the forests.

_____ Score 15 points for a correct M answer.

_____ Score 5 points for each correct B or N answer.

_____ **Total Score:** Finding the Main Idea

B Recalling Facts

How well do you remember the facts in the article? Put an X in the box next to the answer that correctly completes each statement about the article.

1. At the age of 15, Marina learned
   - ☐ a. how to tap rubber trees.
   - ☐ b. enough arithmetic to protect the family business.
   - ☐ c. how to read and write.

2. Marina could no longer do the work involved in tapping rubber trees because she
   - ☐ a. had been weakened by hepatitis.
   - ☐ b. was working as a maid.
   - ☐ c. was attending classes in a big city.

3. Marina joined forces with Chico Mendes to
   - ☐ a. protect the rain forests from the rubber tappers.
   - ☐ b. earn a college degree in history.
   - ☐ c. fight the ranchers who were destroying the rain forests.

4. On December 22, 1988,
   - ☐ a. a rancher tried to kill Marina.
   - ☐ b. a rancher murdered Chico.
   - ☐ c. the government set aside over four million acres of Amazonia as reserves.

5. As a reward for her efforts to protect the rain forests, Marina
   - ☐ a. won the Amazon Legend Award.
   - ☐ b. won the Goldman Environmental Award.
   - ☐ c. was elected to the Brazilian Federal Senate.

Score 5 points for each correct answer.

_____ **Total Score:** Recalling Facts

C **Making Inferences**

When you combine your own experience and information from a text to draw a conclusion that is not directly stated in that text, you are making an inference. Below are five statements that may or may not be inferences based on information in the article. Label the statements using the following key:

C—Correct Inference   F—Faulty Inference

_____ 1. Marina was a fast learner and a hard worker.

_____ 2. The rubber tappers did not take Marina seriously because she was a woman.

_____ 3. Marina was desperate to leave the rain forest so that she could get a good education.

_____ 4. The ranchers working in the rain forests made more money than the rubber tappers.

_____ 5. Chico Mendes is considered a hero in Brazil.

Score 5 points for each correct answer.

_____ **Total Score:** Making Inferences

D **Using Words Precisely**

Each numbered sentence below contains an underlined word or phrase from the article. Following the sentence are three definitions. One definition is closest to the meaning of the underlined word. One definition is opposite or nearly opposite. Label those two definitions using the following key. Do not label the remaining definition.

C—Closest   O—Opposite or Nearly Opposite

1. For her, the forests were not just some <u>exotic</u> tourist spot.

_____ a. ordinary

_____ b. expensive

_____ c. excitingly different

2. Soon she could no longer go out and do the <u>strenuous</u> work involved in tapping rubber trees.

_____ a. requiring a great deal of energy

_____ b. requiring a small amount of work

_____ c. requiring a great deal of time

3. Soon, Marina realized, the place where she grew up would be a <u>wasteland</u>.

_____ a. a lush paradise

_____ b. a garbage dump

_____ c. an empty wilderness

4. The ranchers, furious at the <u>obstruction</u>, tried to get the people to move.

_____ a. assistance

_____ b. barrier

_____ c. demonstration

5. She won the <u>prestigious</u> Goldman Environmental Award.

_____ a. highly regarded

_____ b. unusual

_____ c. dishonorable

_____ Score 3 points for each correct C answer.

_____ Score 2 points for each correct O answer.

_____ **Total Score:** Using Words Precisely

Enter the four total scores in the spaces below, and add them together to find your Reading Comprehension Score. Then record your score on the graph on page 135.

Score	Question Type	Lesson 9
_____	Finding the Main Idea	
_____	Recalling Facts	
_____	Making Inferences	
_____	Using Words Precisely	
_____	**Reading Comprehension Score**	

Author's Approach

Put an X in the box next to the correct answer.

1. What does the author mean by the statement "Where others saw sickness, however, Marina saw opportunity"?

☐ a. Marina made the best of what others might consider a bad situation.

☐ b. Marina was glad she was sick.

☐ c. Marina's illness caused her to see things.

2. From the statements below, choose those that you believe the author would agree with.

☐ a. If he had lived, Chico Mendes would have been jealous of Marina's fame and recognition.

☐ b. Marina Silva was ready to die for the movement.

☐ c. The ranchers were willing to sacrifice the rain forests for profits.

3. Choose the statement below that is the weakest argument for saving the rain forests.

☐ a. Destruction of the rain forests will put the ranchers and loggers out of business.

☐ b. Destruction of the rain forests will leave behind a wasteland that cannot support the animals that live there.

☐ c. Destruction of the rain forests will ruin the rubber tappers and their way of life.

4. How is the author's purpose for writing the article expressed in paragraph 13?

☐ a. The author reveals the ranchers' violent tactics.

☐ b. The author explains that Marina decided to continue her fight, even in the face of personal danger.

☐ c. The author informs the reader about key events in the movement to save the rain forests.

_____ Number of correct answers

Record your personal assessment of your work on the Critical Thinking Chart on page 136.

Summarizing and Paraphrasing

Put an X in the box next to the correct answer for question 2. Follow the directions provided for the other question.

1. Reread paragraph 9 in the article. Below, write a summary of the paragraph in no more than 25 words.

_____

_____

_____

Reread your summary and decide if the summary covers important parts of the paragraph. Next, decide how to shorten the summary to 15 words or less without leaving out any essential information. Write this summary below.

_____

_____

_____

2. Read the statement about the article below. Then read the paraphrase of that statement. Choose the reason that best tells why the paraphrase does not say the same thing as the statement.

Statement: People throughout the world supported the rubber tappers and pressured the Brazilian government to protect the rain forests.

Paraphrase: World opinion backed Marina Silva and her movement.

☐ a. Paraphrase says too much.

☐ b. Paraphrase doesn't say enough.

☐ c. Paraphrase doesn't agree with the statement about the article.

_____ Number of correct answers

Record your personal assessment of your work on the Critical Thinking Chart on page 136.

Critical Thinking

Put an X in the box next to the correct answer for questions 1, 4, and 5. Follow the directions provided for the other questions.

1. Based on what the article told about Marina Silva, you can predict that she will
   - ☐ a.   be elected president of Brazil.
   - ☐ b.   return home and become a rubber tapper.
   - ☐ c.   continue to fight for her people.

2. Choose from the letters below to correctly complete the following statement. Write the letters on the lines.

   In the article, _____ and _____ are different.
   - a.   the rubber tappers
   - b.   the ranchers
   - c.   the seringueiros

3. Choose from the letters below to correctly complete the following statement. Write the letters on the lines.

   According to the article, the empates caused _____ to _____, and the effect was _____.
   - a.   Marina's refusal to back down
   - b.   Darcy Alves
   - c.   murder Chico Mendes

4. Of the following theme categories, which would this story fit into?
   - ☐ a.   One person can make a difference.
   - ☐ b.   Greed can overcome reason.
   - ☐ c.   Love can triumph over hate.

5. What did you have to do to answer question 1?
   - ☐ a.   find a fact (something that you can prove is true)
   - ☐ b.   draw a conclusion (a sensible statement based on the text and your experience)
   - ☐ c.   find a contrast (how things are different)

_____ Number of correct answers

Record your personal assessment of your work on the Critical Thinking Chart on page 136.

Personal Response

What new question do you have about this topic?

_____

_____

Self-Assessment

I was confused on question number _____ in section _____ because

_____

_____

CRITICAL THINKING

ANNE & CHARLES LINDBERGH
Opening the Skies

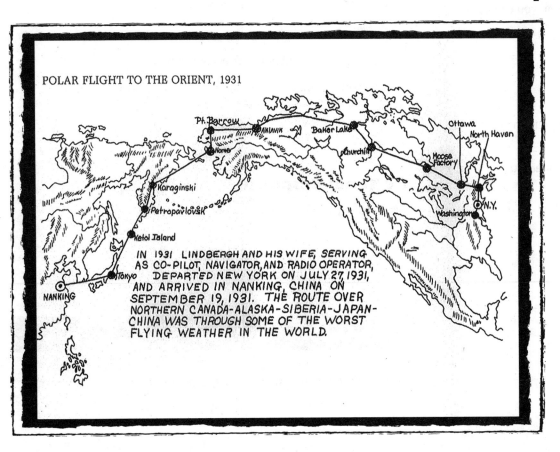

POLAR FLIGHT TO THE ORIENT, 1931

IN 1931 LINDBERGH AND HIS WIFE, SERVING AS CO-PILOT, NAVIGATOR, AND RADIO OPERATOR, DEPARTED NEW YORK ON JULY 27, 1931, AND ARRIVED IN NANKING, CHINA ON SEPTEMBER 19, 1931. THE ROUTE OVER NORTHERN CANADA-ALASKA-SIBERIA-JAPAN-CHINA WAS THROUGH SOME OF THE WORST FLYING WEATHER IN THE WORLD.

A map showing the route the Lindberghs followed from New York City to Nanking, China

He was the most famous person in the world. She was the daughter of the American ambassador to Mexico. In 1927, he became the first pilot to fly nonstop across the Atlantic Ocean, traveling from New York to Paris. She knew nothing about airplanes or flying. He loved cars, planes—anything that went fast. She loved books and hoped one day to become a writer. Charles and Anne Lindbergh seemed to have little in common. Yet together they wrote some of the most important pages in the history of aviation.

2   Anne and Charles married in 1929. Charles made it clear from the beginning that he did not want his wife to sit at home while he was off flying. If they were going to be married, they were going to be a team. Anne would have to learn to use Morse Code and to operate a two-way radio. She would also have to learn how to navigate. She did all of that gladly. Wherever Charles decided to fly, Anne was prepared to be right there in the cockpit with him.

3   In 1931, the Lindberghs got their first big opportunity to work together. Charles, who was a technical consultant for Pan American Airways, was contacted by Juan Trippe, the company's founder. Trippe asked the Lindberghs to survey an air

route from the United States to Asia. The route was a great circle route. A great circle route is the shortest distance between two points on the earth's surface. This particular route ran over Canada, across Alaska, and down to Japan and China. It was the shortest distance between the east coast of North America and the Orient.

4   No one had ever flown the route before, and many pilots doubted that it could be done. Pilots familiar with the Arctic urged Charles and Anne not to try it. They pointed out the dangerous weather conditions that prevailed along the route. Storms and fog sprang up without warning. There were no landing strips, supply stations, or refueling pads along the way. For much of the trip the Lindberghs would be out of radio contact with the rest of the world. And near the North Pole the pull from the magnetic pole would make their compass worthless.

5   The Lindberghs listened as the pilots ran down the list of dangers. But in the end they decided to make the attempt anyway. Charles, eager for new challenges, believed that if they planned the trip carefully enough they could make it. Once that decision was made, he and Anne began preparing for the journey.

6   To begin with, they bought the best plane available. It was a seaplane, which meant it was equipped with pontoons for water landings. With a top speed of 185 miles per hour, it was one of the fastest planes of its day. When the Lindberghs saw the plane, they decided to name it *Sirius,* after the brightest star in the sky.

7   The sleek black and red *Sirius* could carry enough gasoline to travel 2,000 miles. The total mileage of the trip, however, was more than 8,000 miles. The Lindberghs, therefore, had to arrange for fuel tanks to be set out along the route. Next they had to decide what supplies to take with them. They packed repair kits and emergency medical supplies. They took parachutes in case they had to abandon the plane. They packed handguns so they could shoot animals if they ran out of food. They brought along matches, rope, and a rubber raft. They even packed special flight suits that could be heated by electricity to ward off the Arctic cold.

8   By July 29, 1931, the Lindberghs were ready. They took off from College Point, Long Island, in New York, and landed in Maine, where they stopped briefly to visit family. From there they went to Ottawa, Canada. On August 1, they left Ottawa and started northwest across the continent. The first part of the trip went smoothly. With Charles at the controls and Anne working the radio, they made good progress. Each day they flew farther and farther north. Each night they landed on a river or lake and dropped anchor. For the first week it seemed that all the dangers they had been warned about were imaginary. But on August 8, as they approached Point Barrow in northern Alaska, things began to go wrong.

9   First they hit a fog so dense that they could see nothing but fine white mist all around them. They managed to land

Anne Morrow Lindbergh and Charles Lindbergh

safely at Point Barrow, but there they found bad news awaiting them. The gasoline they had ordered had not yet reached the tiny coastal town. They had no way to refuel. After discussing the situation, Anne and Charles decided to keep going, rather than wait for the fuel to reach them. Charles figured the *Sirius* had just enough fuel left to make it to Nome, Alaska.

10   On the afternoon of August 11, the Lindberghs left Point Barrow and headed southwest toward the small mining town of Nome. They expected it would take about seven hours to get there. Ordinarily they would not have left so late in the day. They didn't want to get caught flying at night over unfamiliar territory. But this time they did not worry. It was summertime and they were in the Arctic. They were sure that the summer sun never set in that part of the world.

11   But Charles and Anne were wrong about the sun. It was true that the Arctic sky never got very dark in June. But this was August. Besides, the Lindberghs were flying south, away from the land of endless summer light. By 8:00 P.M. it was clear that the sun was going down. By 8:30 it had gotten so dark that Anne could barely read the note her husband handed her. The message read, "What time does it get dark in Nome?"

12   Quickly Anne went to work on the radio. She had to contact Nome. She needed to find out if there would be enough daylight left for them to land on the Nome River as planned. They were still almost two hours from Nome, and the *Sirius* was running low on gas. They didn't have the time or the fuel to look for another landing spot.

13   The radio operator in Nome sent back a message that was not encouraging. It was already getting dark there. The radio operator offered to put flares out along the Nome River, but still the Lindberghs would be landing in the dark.

14   Both Charles and Anne knew that they should not do that. It was simply too dangerous. They didn't know the exact width, depth, or contour of the river. If they tried to land there in the dark, they might injure themselves or the plane. They decided to make a forced landing somewhere and wait until morning to fly into Nome. They had to hurry; it was getting darker every second. Anne radioed Nome to tell the radio operator their plan. Then Charles sent the plane plunging through the clouds and mist toward an ocean inlet. Somehow he managed to land the *Sirius* safely in the small patch of calm water. Not until the plane had landed did the Lindberghs realize the water in the inlet was only three feet deep.

15   The next morning, recovered from their close call, Charles and Anne continued their journey. They stopped briefly in Nome to refuel the *Sirius*. As they traveled farther along their course, they ran into many other frightening situations. At one point the fog became incredibly thick. In order to see anything at all, they had to fly up and down the sides of mountains, very close to treetops and rocky ledges. Terrified, Anne felt sure they were going to crash. To her, it seemed the plane had suddenly become "like a knife going down the side of a pie tin, between fog and mountains." At another point, bad weather forced them to fly so low that the *Sirius* actually did skip across the treetops. In the course of the trip, they made three emergency landings.

16   Despite all the difficulties, however, on September 19, 1931, the Lindberghs landed in China. That ended their long and dangerous journey. They had successfully flown where no one else had dared to go. They had proved that it was possible to fly the great circle route from New York to the Orient. In the years that followed, the Lindberghs went on to pioneer other air routes. By the time their flying careers ended, Charles and Anne Lindbergh had changed the way people looked at aviation. 🍃

If you have been timed while reading this article, enter your reading time below. Then turn to the Words-per-Minute Table on page 133 and look up your reading speed (words per minute). Enter your reading speed on the graph on page 134.

Reading Time: Lesson 10

_____ : _____

Minutes   Seconds

A Finding the Main Idea

One statement below expresses the main idea of the article. One statement is too general, or too broad. The other statement explains only part of the article; it is too narrow. Label the statements using the following key:

M—Main Idea　　　**B—Too Broad**　　　**N—Too Narrow**

_____　1. Charles and Anne Lindbergh met with great difficulties as they flew across Alaska.

_____　2. Charles and Anne Lindbergh were among the world's greatest aviation pioneers.

_____　3. Charles and Anne Lindbergh were the first aviators to fly the dangerous great circle route from New York to the Orient.

_____　Score 15 points for a correct M answer.

_____　Score 5 points for each correct B or N answer.

_____　**Total Score:** Finding the Main Idea

B Recalling Facts

How well do you remember the facts in the article? Put an X in the box next to the answer that correctly completes each statement about the article.

1. Anne Lindbergh's early desire was to become a
   - ☐ a. pilot.
   - ☐ b. radio operator.
   - ☐ c. writer.

2. *Sirius,* the Lindberghs' plane, was named after
   - ☐ a. the brightest star in the sky.
   - ☐ b. a city in China.
   - ☐ c. the founder of Pan American Airways.

3. The Lindberghs were running out of both gas and daylight on their way to
   - ☐ a. Nome, Alaska.
   - ☐ b. Point Barrow, Alaska.
   - ☐ c. Ottawa, Canada.

4. The greatest danger the Lindberghs faced while flying to Nome was
   - ☐ a. an Arctic storm.
   - ☐ b. approaching darkness.
   - ☐ c. a useless compass.

5. The ocean inlet that the Lindberghs were forced to land on was only
   - ☐ a. three inches deep.
   - ☐ b. three feet deep.
   - ☐ c. six inches deep.

Score 5 points for each correct answer.

_____　**Total Score:** Recalling Facts

C Making Inferences

When you combine your own experience and information from a text to draw a conclusion that is not directly stated in that text, you are making an inference. Below are five statements that may or may not be inferences based on information in the article. Label the statements using the following key:

C—Correct Inference   **F—Faulty Inference**

_____ 1. Anne Lindbergh would not have become an important pioneer in aviation if she had not married Charles Lindbergh.

_____ 2. The survey of the great circle route from New York to China was the first dangerous flight Charles Lindbergh had ever made.

_____ 3. The Lindberghs would not have found themselves in such dangerous situations if they had planned their trip more carefully.

_____ 4. The Lindbergh's flight from New York to the Orient helped to open up the skies for the growing business of aviation.

_____ 5. The great circle route across the Arctic is still a difficult and dangerous route to fly.

Score 5 points for each correct answer.

_____ **Total Score:** Making Inferences

D Using Words Precisely

Each numbered sentence below contains an underlined word or phrase from the article. Following the sentence are three definitions. One definition is closest to the meaning of the underlined word. One definition is opposite or nearly opposite. Label those two definitions using the following key. Do not label the remaining definition.

C—Closest   O—Opposite or Nearly Opposite

1. Trippe asked the Lindberghs to <u>survey</u> an air route from the United States to Asia.

_____ a. alter

_____ b. avoid

_____ c. explore

2. Charles, <u>eager</u> for new challenges, believed that if they planned the trip carefully enough, they could make it.

_____ a. anxious

_____ b. lazy

_____ c. uninterested

3. They even packed special flight suits heated by electricity to <u>ward off</u> the Arctic cold.

_____ a. attract

_____ b. keep away

_____ c. heat up

4. They decided to make a <u>forced</u> landing somewhere and wait until morning to fly into Nome.

_____ a. violent

_____ b. unnecessary

_____ c. required

5. Then Charles sent the plane <u>plunging</u> through the clouds and mist toward an ocean inlet.

_____ a. flying

_____ b. diving headlong

_____ c. rising straight up

_____ Score 3 points for each correct C answer.

_____ Score 2 points for each correct O answer.

_____ **Total Score:** Using Words Precisely

Enter the four total scores in the spaces below, and add them together to find your Reading Comprehension Score. Then record your score on the graph on page 135.

Score	Question Type	Lesson 10
_____	Finding the Main Idea	
_____	Recalling Facts	
_____	Making Inferences	
_____	Using Words Precisely	
_____	**Reading Comprehension Score**	

Author's Approach

Put an X in the box next to the correct answer.

1. The main purpose of the first paragraph is to
   - ☐ a. inform the reader about the history of aviation.
   - ☐ b. emphasize the similarities between Anne and Charles Lindbergh.
   - ☐ c. emphasize the differences between Anne and Charles Lindbergh.

2. Which of the following statements from the article best describes the Lindberghs?
   - ☐ a. "If they were going to be married, they were going to be a team."
   - ☐ b. "Charles and Anne Lindbergh seemed to have little in common."
   - ☐ c. "With Charles at the controls and Anne working the radio, they made good progress."

3. The author probably wrote this article in order to
   - ☐ a. relate the love story between Charles and Anne Lindbergh.
   - ☐ b. describe the dangerous conditions of their flight to Asia.
   - ☐ c. tell readers about the Lindberghs' impact on aviation.

_____ Number of correct answers

Record your personal assessment of your work on the Critical Thinking Chart on page 136.

CRITICAL THINKING

Summarizing and Paraphrasing

Put an X in the box next to the correct answer for question 3. Follow the directions provided for the other questions.

1. Complete the following one-sentence summary of the article using the lettered phrases from the phrase bank below. Write the letters on the lines.

> **Phrase Bank:**
> a. their successful arrival in China after weathering many dangers
> b. their decision to fly to Asia
> c. a description of their relationship

The article about Charles and Anne Lindbergh begins with _____, goes on to explain _____, and ends with _____.

2. Reread paragraph 14 in the article. Below, write a summary of the paragraph in no more than 25 words.

_____

_____

_____

_____

Reread your summary and decide if the summary covers important parts of the paragraph. Next, decide how to shorten the summary to 15 words or less without leaving out any essential information. Write this summary below.

_____

_____

3. Choose the sentence that correctly restates the following sentence from the article:

    "To her, it seemed the plane had suddenly become 'like a knife going down the side of a pie tin, between fog and mountains.'"

☐ a. The plane cut through the side of a mountain.

☐ b. The plane sliced through the fog that covered the sides of the mountains.

☐ c. The sides of the plane were sharp enough to cut through tin.

> _____ Number of correct answers
>
> Record your personal assessment of your work on the Critical Thinking Chart on page 136.

Critical Thinking

Put an X in the box next to the correct answer for questions 1, 3, 4, and 5. Follow the directions provided for the other question.

1. Based on what the article told about the Lindberghs, you can predict that they will

☐ a. continue to work together as a team.

☐ b. try to find a better route to Asia.

☐ c. refuse to fly dangerous routes again.

2. Using what you know about the Lindberghs and what is told about them in the article, name three ways Charles Lindbergh is similar to and three ways he is different from Anne Lindbergh. Cite the paragraph number(s) where you found details in the article to support your conclusions.

Similarities

_____

_____

_____

Differences

_____

_____

_____

3. What was the effect of leaving Point Barrow so late in the day?

☐ a. The Lindberghs' plane ran out of gas.

☐ b. The radio operator put out flares along the Nome River so that the Lindberghs could land in the dark.

☐ c. The Lindberghs couldn't land in Nome because it got too dark.

4. What was the cause of having to fly over the Arctic to reach China?

☐ a. It was the safest route.

☐ b. It was the only route.

☐ c. It was the shortest route.

5. If you were a pilot working today, how could you use the information in the article to fly an unknown route?

☐ a. Like the Lindberghs, never fly at night.

☐ b. Like the Lindberghs, keep in constant contact with radio operators where you plan to land.

☐ c. Like the Lindberghs, fly at a top speed of 185 miles per hour.

_____ Number of correct answers

Record your personal assessment of your work on the Critical Thinking Chart on page 136.

Personal Response

How do you think you would feel if you were flying a plane and knew you had to make a forced landing?

_____

_____

_____

_____

Self-Assessment

I'm proud of how I answered question number _____ in section _____ because

_____

_____

_____

_____

CRITICAL THINKING

THE CREW OF FLIGHT 847
Terror in the Air

The hijacked TWA Flight 847 sits on a runway at the airport in Beirut, Lebanon, June 22, 1985.

TWA Flight 847 had just lifted off from Athens, Greece, on June 14, 1985. For the 8-member crew and 145 passengers, the trip was supposed to be a routine hop to Rome, Italy. But it didn't work out that way. Less than 20 minutes into the flight, two Muslim terrorists, brandishing a pistol and holding grenades, took over the plane.

2   One used a karate kick on head flight attendant Uli Derickson. He slammed her against the cockpit door. Then he brought the muzzle of his gun to her left temple. The other terrorist banged on the cockpit door. "We come to die, we come to die," he shouted. "Open the door. We come to die."

3   The door opened, and the two terrorists stormed inside. One of the gunmen began to beat flight engineer Benjamin Zimmerman with his pistol. The other gunman screamed at Captain John

Testrake, the pilot. "Beirut! Beirut!" he shouted.

4   Testrake, with a gun pointed at his head, made a steep turn to reverse course. He headed for Beirut, Lebanon. When he got there, Beirut officials wanted nothing to do with a skyjacked plane. They refused to let the plane land. To prove their point, they blocked the runway with buses. Testrake, however, knew how deadly serious the terrorists were. He had to land. "We must land in Beirut. [One of the gunmen] has pulled the pin of the grenade," Testrake radioed to Lebanese officials. "We must land. He is ready to blow up the plane!"

5   At last, officials let the plane land. The terrorists then let the world know what they wanted. They demanded that Israel release over 700 prisoners, most of whom were Muslims. The Israelis and their Muslim neighbors had been fighting on and off since Israel officially came into existence in 1948. Sadly, terrorism had become a part of life in the Middle East.

6   After the plane landed, Derickson pleaded for the lives of the women and children on board. At first, the gunmen refused to listen to her. But Derickson bravely persisted. She begged them to let at least the old women and young children go. Finally, the terrorists agreed. They chose 18 people whom they were

willing to release. One was a 4-year-old girl who was sleeping in her mother's arms. When the terrorists indicated that the mother had to stay, Derickson again spoke up. She told the terrorists they could not send a small child off into a strange country without her mother. Once again, Derickson's boldness paid off. The mother, child, and 17 others got off the plane.

7   The gunmen then ordered Testrake to fly to Algiers, Algeria. Officials there didn't want anything to do with the plane, either. But they, too, let it land after an urgent plea from U.S. president Ronald Reagan. The Boeing 727 refueled in Algiers, and 21 more passengers were released. Then the skyjackers told Testrake to fly back to Beirut.

8   By this time, of course, the passengers were numb with fear. It had been 12 hours since the gunmen had taken over. During that time, the terrorists had been constantly threatening to blow the entire plane to bits. To make matters worse, no one could figure out why the terrorists kept having the plane fly between Beirut and Algiers.

9   As the weary Testrake flew back to Beirut, the gunmen singled out a few passengers. One was an American serviceman, a 23-year-old navy diver named Robert Stethem. The terrorists, who felt that the United States didn't support

Muslims in the Middle East, hated all Americans. That included Stethem. They tied Stethem's wrists behind his back so tightly that his hands turned white. Then one of the terrorists blindfolded him. They began to beat him with an armrest.

10   Uli Derickson stood just a few feet away. She later described the torture. "They were jumping in the air and landing full force on his body," she said. "He must have had all his ribs broken. They put the mike up to his face so his

U. S. Navy diver Robert Stethem who was murdered by the hijackers of TWA Flight 847

screams could be heard by the outside world."

11   After they finished, Derickson tried to comfort Stethem. One of the terrorists waved her away, saying, "No. Leave him alone. He's just an American pig."

12   The gunmen then started beating Clinton Suggs, another U.S. serviceman. Derickson couldn't take it anymore. She threw herself between the gunmen and Suggs. "We are cooperating," she cried. "We are doing everything you want. Stop it right now." Amazingly, her heroism paid off. The gunman backed away.

13   Once again, the Beirut officials did not want Flight 847 to land. The control tower refused to give them clearance or any landing instructions. Testrake radioed that he was running low on fuel. He could only stay in the air another six minutes. In addition, the terrorists had threatened to kill him if he did not land the plane.

14   One of the terrorists shouted over the radio, "We are suicide terrorists! If you don't let us land, we will crash the plane into your control tower, or crash into the Presidential Palace!" The Lebanese decided they had no choice. They agreed to let the plane land.

15   Captain Testrake informed the passengers that they would soon be on the ground again. He kept his voice calm as he announced, "Ladies and gentlemen, it will be a normal landing." The gunmen also told Derickson to announce that there would be a noise after they landed. That noise turned out to be a pistol shot. Upon landing, the terrorists shot Robert Stethem in the back of the head. They dumped his lifeless body out the door onto the tarmac.

16   One passenger later remembered Stethem's courage. "He believed that someone would die on the plane, someone from the navy men," said Ruth Henderson. "He said because he was the only one who wasn't married, that he should be the one to die."

17   In Beirut, 10 more terrorists joined the two gunmen. These 10 had taken over the airport and gained access to the skyjacked plane. With them aboard, Testrake was again ordered to fly to Algiers.

18   During their second stopover in Algiers, the terrorists released 61 passengers and crew members. One was Uli Derickson, who had mixed emotions about her release. On the one hand, she was happy to get off the plane. There had been many times during the past two days when she'd thought she would never see her husband and son again. On the other hand, she was reluctant to go. She felt a duty to remain with the plane. She knew she was leaving hostages behind and that, she said, "made me sick to my stomach."

19   Although the crisis was over for Derickson, it continued for Testrake and the 38 other American men still on the plane. For the next 15 days, they were at the mercy of the terrorists. Testrake was ordered to fly the plane back to Beirut for a third time. Then the gunmen took him and the others off the plane and hid them somewhere in the city. The world waited in anguish to see what would happen next.

20   At last, on June 30, the terrorists released all the remaining hostages. Israel, meanwhile, began to release its Muslim prisoners. The United States denied that there was any link between Israel's action and the release of the hostages.

21   Safely home, Captain John Testrake and Uli Derickson were welcomed as heroes. People cheered Testrake for keeping his cool with a gun pointed at his head. They applauded Derickson for her courage in standing up to the terrorists. Later, a made-for-TV movie told her amazing story.

22   Robert Stethem, the other hero, was the sole casualty of the crisis. He, too, was well remembered. In 1995, a new navy ship was named for him. At that time, President Bill Clinton summed up what everyone felt. "Stethem was a true American hero," the President wrote. "This ship will sail in the defense of freedom around the world, reminding us all of Robert's legacy of heroism." 🍃

If you have been timed while reading this article, enter your reading time below. Then turn to the Words-per-Minute Table on page 133 and look up your reading speed (words per minute). Enter your reading speed on the graph on page 134.

Reading Time: Lesson 11

_____ : _____
Minutes   *Seconds*

A Finding the Main Idea

One statement below expresses the main idea of the article. One statement is too general, or too broad. The other statement explains only part of the article; it is too narrow. Label the statements using the following key:

M—Main Idea   **B—Too Broad**   **N—Too Narrow**

_____ 1. Terrorists skyjacked a plane and held frightened passengers hostage for several days.

_____ 2. Muslim terrorists skyjacked a plane and killed U.S. serviceman Robert Stethem.

_____ 3. Flight attendant Uli Derickson and pilot John Testrake showed great courage after Muslim terrorists skyjacked their plane and held the passengers and crew hostage.

_____ Score 15 points for a correct M answer.

_____ Score 5 points for each correct B or N answer.

_____ **Total Score:** Finding the Main Idea

B Recalling Facts

How well do you remember the facts in the article? Put an X in the box next to the answer that correctly completes each statement about the article.

1. When the terrorists first took over the plane, they demanded that the pilot fly to
   ☐ a. Beirut, Lebanon.
   ☐ b. Algiers, Algeria.
   ☐ c. Israel.

2. Derickson begged the terrorists to let
   ☐ a. the old women and young children go.
   ☐ b. her go.
   ☐ c. the navy men go.

3. Algerian officials allowed the plane to land after
   ☐ a. the terrorists threatened to blow the plane up with a hand grenade.
   ☐ b. receiving a plea from President Ronald Reagan.
   ☐ c. Israel began to release its Muslim prisoners.

4. The terrorists brutally beat and killed a U.S. serviceman named
   ☐ a. Benjamin Zimmerman.
   ☐ b. Clinton Suggs.
   ☐ c. Robert Stethem.

5. After Derickson was released, the hostage crisis continued for
   ☐ a. two more days.
   ☐ b. fifteen more days.
   ☐ c. one more day.

   Score 5 points for each correct answer.

   _____ **Total Score:** Recalling Facts

C | Making Inferences

When you combine your own experience and information from a text to draw a conclusion that is not directly stated in that text, you are making an inference. Below are five statements that may or may not be inferences based on information in the article. Label the statements using the following key:

C—Correct Inference   **F—Faulty Inference**

_____ 1. All of the Muslims in the Middle East hate Americans.

_____ 2. Uli Derickson was mainly concerned for her own safety.

_____ 3. The terrorists who skyjacked Flight 847 were willing to sacrifice their own lives for their cause.

_____ 4. Terrorist acts occur frequently in the Middle East.

_____ 5. Most governments, even those in the Middle East, do not support terrorists or terrorism.

Score 5 points for each correct answer.

_____ **Total Score:** Making Inferences

D | Using Words Precisely

Each numbered sentence below contains an underlined word or phrase from the article. Following the sentence are three definitions. One definition is closest to the meaning of the underlined word. One definition is opposite or nearly opposite. Label those two definitions using the following key. Do not label the remaining definition.

C—Closest   O—Opposite or Nearly Opposite

1. Less than 20 minutes into the flight, two Muslim terrorists, brandishing a pistol and holding grenades, took over the plane.

_____ a. firing

_____ b. concealing

_____ c. waving

2. But Derickson bravely persisted.

_____ a. stood firm

_____ b. helped others

_____ c. backed down

3. "We are cooperating," she cried.

_____ a. operating a plane

_____ b. working with others

_____ c. unwilling to get along

4. The world waited in anguish to see what would happen next.

_____ a. elation

_____ b. impatience

_____ c. great distress

5. Robert Stethem, the other hero, was the sole <u>casualty</u> of the crisis.

_____ a. survivor

_____ b. dead person

_____ c. witness

_____ Score 3 points for each correct C answer.

_____ Score 2 points for each correct O answer.

_____ **Total Score:** Using Words Precisely

Enter the four total scores in the spaces below, and add them together to find your Reading Comprehension Score. Then record your score on the graph on page 135.

Score	Question Type	Lesson 11
_____	Finding the Main Idea	
_____	Recalling Facts	
_____	Making Inferences	
_____	Using Words Precisely	
_____	**Reading Comprehension Score**	

Author's Approach

Put an X in the box next to the correct answer.

1. The main purpose of the first paragraph is to

☐ a. describe a frightening situation.

☐ b. inform the reader about terrorism in the Middle East.

☐ c. express an opinion about terrorism in the Middle East.

2. Which of the following statements from the article best describes Robert Stethem?

☐ a. "'He said that because he was the only one who wasn't married, that he should be the one to die."

☐ b. "One was an American serviceman, a 23-year-old navy diver named Robert Stethem."

☐ c. "Robert Stethem, the other hero, was the sole casualty of the crisis."

3. Based on the statement from the article, "She felt a duty to remain with the plane," you can conclude that the author wants the reader to think that Uli Derickson

☐ a. felt guilty that she was being released.

☐ b. resented her duties as a flight attendant.

☐ c. felt a great deal of concern for the remaining passengers.

4. The author tells this story mainly by

☐ a. telling different stories about the same topic.

☐ b. retelling personal experiences.

☐ c. using his or her imagination and creativity.

_____ Number of correct answers

Record your personal assessment of your work on the Critical Thinking Chart on page 136.

Summarizing and Paraphrasing

Put an X in the box next to the correct answer for question 3. Follow the directions provided for the other questions.

1. Look for the important ideas and events in paragraphs 9 and 10. Summarize those paragraphs in one or two sentences.

_____

_____

_____

2. Complete the following one-sentence summary of the article using the lettered phrases from the phrase bank below. Write the letters on the lines.

> **Phrase Bank:**
> a. the skyjacking of the plane by Muslim terrorists
> b. the release of the remaining hostages
> c. the passengers' ordeal and the bravery of Derickson, Testrake, and Stethem

The article about Flight 847 begins with _____, goes on to explain _____, and ends with _____.

3. Choose the best one-sentence paraphrase for the following sentence from the article:

"These 10 had taken over the airport and gained access to the skyjacked plane."

☐ a. The 10 terrorists had gained control of the airport and spoke by radio to people on the plane.

☐ b. The 10 terrorists were attacking people in the airport and on the plane.

☐ c. The 10 terrorists had gained control of the airport and boarded the plane.

_____ Number of correct answers

Record your personal assessment of your work on the Critical Thinking Chart on page 136.

Critical Thinking

Put an X in the box next to the correct answer for questions 1, 2, and 4. Follow the directions provided for the other question.

1. Which of the following statements from the article is an opinion rather than a fact?

☐ a. "Sadly, terrorism had become a part of life in the Middle East."

☐ b. "'He's just an American pig.'"

☐ c. "The terrorists, who felt that the United States didn't support Muslims in the Middle East, hated all Americans."

2. Based on what the article told about terrorism in the Middle East, you can predict that

☐ a. terrorists will treat Americans with more respect.

☐ b. terrorist acts will no longer be tolerated in that region.

☐ c. terrorist acts will continue in that region.

3. Choose from the letters below to correctly complete the following statement. Write the letters on the lines.

In the article, _____ and _____ are different.

a. the gunmen aboard Flight 847

b. Muslim terrorists

c. the Lebanese government

4. How is Uli Derickson an example of a hero?

☐ a. She refused to leave the plane until all the other hostages were released.

☐ b. She died trying to save others.

☐ c. She fought to save others.

_____ Number of correct answers

Record your personal assessment of your work on the Critical Thinking Chart on page 136.

Personal Response

I wonder why

_____

_____

_____

Self-Assessment

One of the things I did best when reading this article was

_____

_____

_____

_____

I believe I did this well because

_____

_____

_____

_____

CRITICAL THINKING

STEVE BIKO
South African Freedom Fighter

The funeral procession of black leader Steve Biko moves through King William's Town, South Africa. Black citizens throughout South Africa mourned the beating death of the activist.

Twenty thousand black people jammed the streets of King William's Town, South Africa. They had come to pay their last respects to the great black leader Steve Biko. Many wept as an ox cart moved through the streets, carrying his coffin to the graveyard. Then, as the coffin was lowered into the ground, the mourners raised their right fists in a show of unity. They pledged to continue the battle Steve had fought. They vowed to win freedom and equality for the black citizens of South Africa. All across the country, millions of other blacks echoed that pledge.

2   Steve Biko had not been the only person fighting for the rights of black South Africans. But from 1967 until his death in 1977, he had been the undisputed leader of that struggle. His political career began at the age of 20, when he decided that he could no longer tolerate the laws of his racist society. Everywhere he and his fellow blacks went, they were treated like dirt.

3   Despite the fact that there were four times as many black people as whites in the Republic of South Africa, whites had

controlled the government for well over a hundred years. To make sure that they could maintain control, they made and enforced laws that kept blacks from having any power. They went to such extremes, in fact, that they kept the black population from having even the most basic civil and human rights.

4   Steve Biko wanted to help change the laws that oppressed the native people of South Africa. Those laws did not allow black people to vote. They kept them from living in the capital city. They forbade them from using the same elevators, beaches, and toilets as whites. Blacks were not even allowed to move from one town to another to look for work.

5   In an effort to change the laws that prevented his people from being full members of society, Steve Biko founded a movement called Black Consciousness. The purpose of the movement was to build a sense of pride among the black South Africans. Steve wanted to teach them that they were just as good as white people. They had been oppressed for so long that many had grown to believe that they were in fact inferior. Steve knew that if his people gained confidence and joined together they could change the racist laws of South Africa. Like Martin Luther King, Jr., in the United States, he opposed the use of violence. He hoped to change the society through peaceful means.

6   To awaken the spirits of his people, Steve wrote pamphlets and delivered speeches. He spoke out against the racist policies of the government. He condemned the white policemen who beat black citizens for no reason. He attacked the rich whites who forced blacks to live in poverty, often on the verge of starvation. But most importantly, he called on black people to stand up for their basic human rights.

7   Because of Steve Biko's work, the Black Consciousness movement spread quickly. Other groups soon sprang up to advance the cause of black pride and racial equality. The largest of the new groups were the Black Peoples' Convention and the all-black South African Students' Organization. The heads of the groups were all dedicated and courageous people. But even to them, Steve was special. They saw him as one of the most inspiring leaders South Africa had ever known.

8   As the Black Consciousness movement grew, government officials became worried. They feared that they might lose control of the country. To prevent that, they ordered the police to begin arresting black leaders. From 1967 to 1977, hundreds of black activists were jailed.

Many were kept in prisons for months without trial. Some were never even charged with committing a crime. The prisoners often suffered beatings by white guards. In 35 cases, guards actually beat black prisoners to death.

9   As Steve Biko's popularity grew, the South African police zeroed in on him. In 1973, they banned his leaflets and ordered him not to make any more speeches. They declared that he could not be quoted and that he could not be in a room with more than one person at a time. They also ordered him to stay within the boundaries

South African activist Steven Biko

of his home town. Finally, they warned him that the security police would be watching his every move. His phone was tapped. The police kept track of all his visitors. And whenever they felt like it, they entered and searched his home.

10   All those measures were meant to keep Steve Biko out of the public spotlight. If he could not communicate with anyone, he could not stir the people to action.

11   But Steve was not willing to quit. Despite the ban, he kept writing pamphlets. He had them smuggled to underground presses and printed without his name on them. With the help of friends and supporters, he was able to travel outside his town. Speaking in a special code, he continued to use the telephone. So in many ways, Steve continued to provide leadership for the Black Consciousness movement. In addition, he kept up his contacts with other black leaders. Since he could not attend public meetings, he invited members of black activist groups to his home one at a time. He gave them advice and encouragement. People were soon traveling from all over South Africa and from many foreign countries for private talks with Steve Biko.

12   Steve knew the risks of disobeying the government. If caught, he would almost certainly spend the rest of his life in jail. But that didn't matter. He had to continue the fight. He felt that the work he was doing was more important than his personal safety. He was prepared to pay any price in the battle to wipe out racial injustice.

13   If Steve Biko didn't give up, however, neither did the South African government. Acting on orders from top officials, the security police arrested Steve 20 times. Each time, they tried to prove that he had committed a crime. But they always had to release him for lack of evidence. The police hoped to catch him breaking an order, but they never succeeded. Often some of Steve's friends acted as lookouts and warned him when the police were coming. Other times, when he was taken by surprise, Steve managed to stall the police while his wife hid illegal papers and pamphlets.

14   Finally the police had had enough. They decided to get rid of Steve Biko one way or another. On August 18, 1977, they arrested him and took him to headquarters. They did not charge him with any crime. They simply forced him out of his car and dragged him to jail. They stripped him of his clothes and put him in leg irons. He remained chained to a wall for several days, while the leg irons cut into his ankles. Then the police hauled him off to be questioned.

15   They grilled him for hours at a time, trying to get him to confess to all sorts of crimes. When he continually refused to cooperate, they began beating him. They struck him over and over again on the head. After the brutal beating, Steve showed signs of serious brain damage. But the signs were ignored until it was too late. On September 12, 1977, while still in police custody, Steve Biko died.

16   The news of Biko's death shocked the entire black community. In response to demands from other black leaders, the South African government reluctantly agreed to conduct an inquiry. At the hearing, ample evidence was presented of police brutality and neglect. Despite the evidence, however, all police officers and government officials were found innocent.

17   For several more years, South Africa remained an oppressive and racist society. Slowly, however, enormous pressure for change began to build. Both within and outside the country, people wanted to end the old racist policies. During the early 1990s, the dam of white rule finally broke. One by one, South Africa repealed its racial laws. In 1994, in a free and open election, Nelson Mandela, once a black nationalist prisoner like Biko, was elected president of South Africa. It was the memory of Steve Biko's inner strength and personal sacrifice that inspired black leaders to help to build a new South Africa. 🍃

If you have been timed while reading this article, enter your reading time below. Then turn to the Words-per-Minute Table on page 133 and look up your reading speed (words per minute). Enter your reading speed on the graph on page 134.

Reading Time: Lesson 12

_____ : _____
Minutes   Seconds

A | Finding the Main Idea

One statement below expresses the main idea of the article. One statement is too general, or too broad. The other statement explains only part of the article; it is too narrow. Label the statements using the following key:

M—Main Idea   **B—Too Broad**   **N—Too Narrow**

_____ 1. Steve Biko was committed to trying to win rights for blacks in South Africa.

_____ 2. Steve Biko died after he was beaten by South African police during a questioning session.

_____ 3. Steve Biko sacrificed his life in an effort to win racial equality for blacks in South Africa.

_____ Score 15 points for a correct M answer.

_____ Score 5 points for each correct B or N answer.

_____ **Total Score:** Finding the Main Idea

B | Recalling Facts

How well do you remember the facts in the article? Put an X in the box next to the answer that correctly completes each statement about the article.

1. In South Africa no black could
   ☐ a. write pamphlets.
   ☐ b. vote.
   ☐ c. be with more than one person at a time.

2. Steve Biko wanted blacks to
   ☐ a. develop a sense of pride.
   ☐ b. fight back when police beat them.
   ☐ c. use violence to change South African racial policy.

3. Steve disobeyed the government's orders because he
   ☐ a. didn't think he would be caught.
   ☐ b. didn't think the police would put him in jail for very long.
   ☐ c. felt his work was too important to be stopped.

4. When Steve was arrested on August 18, 1977, he
   ☐ a. immediately confessed to going against the government's orders.
   ☐ b. used a special code to telephone his family.
   ☐ c. was stripped of his clothes and put in chains.

5. As a result of the investigation into Steve Biko's death,
   ☐ a. policy towards blacks began to change.
   ☐ b. neither the government nor the police were found guilty.
   ☐ c. the police were found guilty of brutality.

Score 5 points for each correct answer.

_____ **Total Score:** Recalling Facts

C | Making Inferences

When you combine your own experience and information from a text to draw a conclusion that is not directly stated in that text, you are making an inference. Below are five statements that may or may not be inferences based on information in the article. Label the statements using the following key:

C—Correct Inference   F—Faulty Inference

_____ 1. If the blacks in South Africa were allowed to vote and to hold political office, whites would still rule the country.

_____ 2. If Steve Biko had lived longer, sooner or later he would have turned to violent means to change South Africa's racial policies.

_____ 3. The South African government feared that Steve's speeches and pamphlets would stir up trouble among blacks.

_____ 4. Steve Biko did not have many friends.

_____ 5. South African police did not beat white prisoners the way they beat black prisoners.

Score 5 points for each correct answer.

_____ **Total Score:** Making Inferences

D | Using Words Precisely

Each numbered sentence below contains an underlined word or phrase from the article. Following the sentence are three definitions. One definition is closest to the meaning of the underlined word. One definition is opposite or nearly opposite. Label those two definitions using the following key. Do not label the remaining definition.

C—Closest   O—Opposite or Nearly Opposite

1. Blacks had been <u>oppressed</u> for so long that many had grown to believe that they were in fact inferior.

_____ a. uneducated

_____ b. assisted

_____ c. kept down

2. He attacked the rich whites who forced blacks to live in poverty, often <u>on the verge</u> of starvation.

_____ a. bordering

_____ b. far from

_____ c. on top of

3. He was prepared to pay any price in the battle to wipe out racial <u>injustice</u>.

_____ a. hatred

_____ b. unfairness

_____ c. equality

4. In response to demands from other black leaders, the South African government <u>reluctantly</u> agreed to conduct an inquiry.

_____ a. enthusiastically

_____ b. unwillingly

_____ c. slowly

5. At the hearing there was <u>ample</u> evidence of police brutality and neglect.

_____ a. plenty of

_____ b. not enough

_____ c. reasonable

_____ Score 3 points for each correct C answer.

_____ Score 2 points for each correct O answer.

_____ **Total Score:** Using Words Precisely

Enter the four total scores in the spaces below, and add them together to find your Reading Comprehension Score. Then record your score on the graph on page 135.

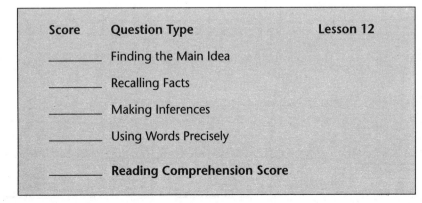

Score	Question Type	Lesson 12
_____	Finding the Main Idea	
_____	Recalling Facts	
_____	Making Inferences	
_____	Using Words Precisely	
_____	**Reading Comprehension Score**	

Author's Approach

Put an X in the box next to the correct answer.

1. The author uses the first sentence of the article to

☐ a. inform the reader about the crowded conditions in South Africa.

☐ b. describe a scene.

☐ c. express an opinion about racial oppression.

2. What does the author mean by the statement "To awaken the spirits of his people, Steve wrote pamphlets and delivered speeches"?

☐ a. Steve often had to wake people up so they could read his writings and listen to his speeches.

☐ b. Through his writings and speeches, Steve became an important spiritual leader in South Africa.

☐ c. Steve used both the written and spoken word to instill pride in South Africans and to encourage them to oppose the country's racial laws.

3. Choose the statement below that best describes the author's position in paragraph 16.

☐ a. The government inquiry into Steve Biko's death ensured that justice was served.

☐ b. The evidence presented in the trial was not strong enough to convict the police.

☐ c. The South African police murdered Steve Biko and were not punished for the crime.

4. The author probably wrote this article in order to

☐ a. inspire the reader with Steve Biko's courage.

☐ b. condemn Steve Biko's murderers.

☐ c. awaken the reader to the cruelty of racial injustice.

_____ Number of correct answers

Record your personal assessment of your work on the Critical Thinking Chart on page 136.

Summarizing and Paraphrasing

Put an X in the box next to the correct answer.

1. Below are summaries of the article. Choose the summary that says all the most important things about the article but in the fewest words.

☐ a. Steve Biko was an important leader in the struggle for the rights of blacks in South Africa.

☐ b. Steve Biko sacrificed his life in the fight against racial injustice in South Africa.

☐ c. Steve Biko was murdered by the South African police because he was an important leader in the fight for racial equality.

2. Choose the sentence that correctly restates the following sentence from the article:

"He was prepared to pay any price in the battle to wipe out racial injustice."

☐ a. He was ready to pay any amount of money in order to end racial inequality.

☐ b. He was ready to use violence in order to end racial inequality.

☐ c. He was willing to die in order to end racial inequality.

_____ Number of correct answers

Record your personal assessment of your work on the Critical Thinking Chart on page 136.

Critical Thinking

Put an X in the box next to the correct answer for questions 2 and 5. Follow the directions provided for the other questions.

1. For each statement below, write O if it expresses an opinion and write F if it expresses a fact.

_____ a. Steve believed in nonviolence as a means of changing society.

_____ b. Nonviolence is the best way to fight injustice.

_____ c. The policemen who arrested Steve intended to kill him.

2. Based on the information in paragraph 16, you can predict that

☐ a. many blacks in South Africa would demand that the police be held accountable for their part in Steve Biko's death.

☐ b. the police officers who arrested Steve would confess their role in his death.

☐ c. most blacks in South Africa would be fearful of protesting the government's racial policies.

3. Choose from the letters below to correctly complete the following statement. Write the letters on the lines.

In the article, _____ and _____ are alike.

a. Steve Biko's attitude toward violence

b. the attitude toward violence of the South African police

c. Martin Luther King, Jr.'s, attitude toward violence

4. Think about cause–effect relationships in the article. Fill in the blanks in the cause–effect chart, drawing from the letters below.

Cause	Effect
_____	The police dragged Steve to jail.
Steve's brain damage was ignored.	_____
The government investigated Steve's death.	_____

a. Steve died in jail.

b. The police were found innocent.

c. Steve continued to fight against South Africa's racial laws.

_____ Number of correct answers

Record your personal assessment of your work on the Critical Thinking Chart on page 136.

Personal Response

What new question do you have about this topic?

_____

_____

_____

_____

Self-Assessment

While reading the article, _____ was the easiest for me

_____

_____

_____

_____

CRITICAL THINKING

THE LITTLE ROCK NINE
Battling Segregation

Fifteen-year-old Elizabeth Eckford hurried to get ready for school. After putting on the new dress she had made, she grabbed her notebook and headed out the door. On the way to the city bus stop, she said a prayer. She wasn't afraid, but she was a little nervous. It was Wednesday, September 4, 1957, and she was on her way to Central High School in Little Rock, Arkansas. She and eight other teenagers were about to become the first black students ever to attend that all-white school.

2   A federal court had ordered Central High to begin admitting black students. Three years earlier, in 1954, the United States Supreme Court had ruled that it was unconstitutional to require black and white students to go to separate public schools. Such a system did not offer equal educational opportunities for everyone. Hundreds of schools had become partially integrated since 1954. But in spite of the Supreme Court ruling, Arkansas had not yet begun to integrate its schools. The order to Central High to open its doors to black students was an order for the state to begin the process of desegregation.

3   The bus dropped Elizabeth off one block from Central High. As she walked toward the school, she saw hundreds of white people surrounding the building. She also saw members of the Arkansas National Guard standing by the doorways.

The Little Rock Nine gather with President Clinton and local officials on the steps of Central High School in Little Rock, Arkansas, on September 25, 1997, the fortieth anniversary of their enrollment in the school.

The guardsmen were holding rifles equipped with bayonets. Elizabeth assumed that the soldiers were there to protect her. She thought they would help her get into the school and make sure no one in the crowd bothered her.

4   As she approached the school, she tried not to notice the people staring at her. Still, she sensed their anger. They didn't want her going to the same school as their white children. Walking toward the school, Elizabeth felt her knees start to shake. Suddenly she wasn't sure she could make it. "It was," she said, "the longest block I ever walked in my whole life."

5   Finally she reached the entrance. She expected the soldiers to move aside and escort her into the building. Instead, they put their bayonets across the doorway and refused to let her enter. Only then did Elizabeth realize why they were there. Orval Faubus, the governor of Arkansas, had defied the court order. He had sent the soldiers to keep her out of the school.

6   Elizabeth became terrified. She didn't know what to do. Just then a member of the white mob cried, "Lynch her! Lynch her!" Elizabeth turned and searched the crowd, trying to find a friendly face. She spotted an old woman with kind-looking eyes. But when Elizabeth walked toward her, the old woman spat on her.

7   Unnerved, Elizabeth began to walk back toward the bus stop. She knew she wouldn't be safe until she could climb onto a bus and get out of the area. As she moved down the street, she kept her head up and her eyes focused straight ahead. She didn't want the crowd to know she was scared. By the time she reached the

Surrounded by bayonet-carrying troops, nine African American students enter Central High School in 1957.

bus stop, the mob was in a frenzy. "Drag her over to this tree!" someone shouted. "Let's take care of the nigger!" screamed another.

8   At that point a white man stepped out of the crowd and went over to Elizabeth. He was a reporter for a Northern newspaper. Patting her on the shoulder, he whispered, "Don't let them see you cry." Elizabeth nodded. She knew how important it was to be strong. Although she was terrified, she managed to appear calm until the bus arrived and carried her home. Only when she saw her mother did she begin to cry.

9   Elizabeth Eckford was not the only one who had to face the angry jeers of the crowd that morning. The eight other black students who showed up at Central High also had to confront the mob. One by one they approached the school, and one by one they were turned away by the guardsmen.

10   For the next two and a half weeks the black students stayed home. They had not given up, though. They were simply waiting for the tempers of the white racists to cool. By Monday, September 23, the soldiers had left Central High. On that day the nine teenagers tried again. They went to the school and entered the building. But white people in the community found out that they were there and soon some of them began to gather outside. By mid-morning there were over a thousand of them. For a while they just milled restlessly about. Then they began to talk of violence. They threatened to break into

the school and drag the black students out. City police arrived and tried to prevent trouble, but by noon the situation was almost out of control. Afraid of what might happen, the principal ordered the black students to leave.

11   Two days later the president of the United States, Dwight Eisenhower, stepped in. Overruling Governor Faubus, he put the National Guard under federal control and ordered 10,000 guardsmen to protect the black students. He also sent in a thousand army paratroopers to walk the black students to their classes. Under tight military control then, the nine teenagers returned to Central High.

12   They were finally safe from the throngs of angry adults, but they still had to face the scorn and hatred of their fellow students. Each day white students found new ways to humiliate them. They spat on them, threw ink at them, and sent them nasty notes. They stole books from their lockers. They stuffed their jackets down toilets.

13   Minnejean Brown was singled out as a favorite target. Everywhere she went, she heard white students laughing at her and calling her names. She often went home bruised after being tripped or pushed down stairs. One day a white girl walked up behind her in the cafeteria and, before Minnejean could move, dumped a bowl of hot soup on her.

14   All year the torment continued. In November, the army paratroopers left, but the National Guard remained to keep the peace and protect the students. The black

students, who became known as the Little Rock Nine, remained lonely and isolated. Yet they never stopped going to Central High School. As one southern college professor said, "I cannot recall that there has ever been a more inspiring demonstration of courage by the children of any race, in any age."

15   At the end of the school year, the black students emerged from Central High exhausted but victorious. They had survived an entire year in the hostile environment of the school. They had opened the way for other black children to begin attending white schools. They had even managed to make a few friends among the white students. When Ernest Green graduated that spring, 14 white students asked to sign his yearbook. "I have admired your courage this year," one of them wrote, "and I'm glad you made it through all right." 🍃

If you have been timed while reading this article, enter your reading time below. Then turn to the Words-per-Minute Table on page 133 and look up your reading speed (words per minute). Enter your reading speed on the graph on page 134.

Reading Time: **Lesson 13**

_____ : _____
Minutes   Seconds

A Finding the Main Idea

One statement below expresses the main idea of the article. One statement is too general, or too broad. The other statement explains only part of the article; it is too narrow. Label the statements using the following key:

M—Main Idea   **B—Too Broad**   **N—Too Narrow**

_____ 1. Nine black teenagers in Little Rock, Arkansas, in 1957 courageously faced the hatred of the white community as they became the first blacks in the state to attend an all-white high school.

_____ 2. Orval Faubus, the governor of Arkansas in 1957, tried everything he could to keep from having to desegregate the public schools of Arkansas.

_____ 3. The first black students to attend white public schools in Arkansas faced severe discrimination because of the great prejudice of the white community against blacks.

_____ Score 15 points for a correct M answer.

_____ Score 5 points for each correct B or N answer.

_____ **Total Score:** Finding the Main Idea

B Recalling Facts

How well do you remember the facts in the article? Put an X in the box next to the answer that correctly completes each statement about the article.

1. The bus dropped Elizabeth Eckford off
   ☐ a. in front of Central High.
   ☐ b. at the back door of Central High.
   ☐ c. one block from Central High.

2. The white man who patted Elizabeth's shoulder and said, "Don't let them see you cry" was
   ☐ a. the principal of Central High.
   ☐ b. a member of the Arkansas National Guard.
   ☐ c. a reporter for a Northern newspaper.

3. Dwight Eisenhower
   ☐ a. supported Governor Faubus's decision.
   ☐ b. ordered army paratroopers to walk the black students to classes.
   ☐ c. told the black students to stay home until the tempers of the white people had cooled.

4. As Ernest Green prepared to graduate, 14 white students
   ☐ a. asked to sign his yearbook.
   ☐ b. threatened to beat him.
   ☐ c. poured ink all over him.

5. By the end of the school year,
   ☐ a. all the black students had left Central High.
   ☐ b. the black students had made a few white friends.
   ☐ c. Governor Orval Faubus had left office.

Score 5 points for each correct answer.

_____ **Total Score:** Recalling Facts

C | Making Inferences

When you combine your own experience and information from a text to draw a conclusion that is not directly stated in that text, you are making an inference. Below are five statements that may or may not be inferences based on information in the article. Label the statements using the following key:

C—Correct Inference   F—Faulty Inference

_____ 1. The parents of the Little Rock Nine did not want their children to attend Central High.

_____ 2. The desegregation of Central High School attracted national attention.

_____ 3. Elizabeth Eckford knew she might run into trouble on her first day at the all-white high school.

_____ 4. Arkansas was the only state that was against the desegregation of its schools.

_____ 5. President Dwight Eisenhower did not have the legal authority to take control of the Arkansas National Guard.

Score 5 points for each correct answer.

_____ **Total Score:** Making Inferences

D | Using Words Precisely

Each numbered sentence below contains an underlined word or phrase from the article. Following the sentence are three definitions. One definition is closest to the meaning of the underlined word. One definition is opposite or nearly opposite. Label those two definitions using the following key. Do not label the remaining definition.

C—Closest   O—Opposite or Nearly Opposite

1. Orval Faubus, the governor of Arkansas, had <u>defied</u> the court order.

_____ a. disobeyed

_____ b. misunderstood

_____ c. supported

2. But they still had to face the <u>scorn</u> and hatred of their fellow students.

_____ a. respect

_____ b. curiosity

_____ c. contempt

3. Each day white students found new ways to <u>humiliate</u> them.

_____ a. degrade

_____ b. honor

_____ c. anger

4. All year the <u>torment</u> continued.

_____ a. prejudice

_____ b. torture

_____ c. kindness

5. The black students, who became known as the Little Rock Nine, remained lonely and <u>isolated</u>.

_____ a. separated

_____ b. united

_____ c. depressed

_____ Score 3 points for each correct C answer.

_____ Score 2 points for each correct O answer.

_____ **Total Score:** Using Words Precisely

Enter the four total scores in the spaces below, and add them together to find your Reading Comprehension Score. Then record your score on the graph on page 135.

Score	Question Type	Lesson 13
_____	Finding the Main Idea	
_____	Recalling Facts	
_____	Making Inferences	
_____	Using Words Precisely	
_____	**Reading Comprehension Score**	

Author's Approach

Put an X in the box next to the correct answer.

1. What is the author's purpose in writing "The Little Rock Nine: Battling Segregation"?

☐ a. To convey a mood about prejudice in the 1950s

☐ b. To tell the reader about early efforts to desegregate schools

☐ c. To emphasize the similarities between white students and black students

2. Which of the following statements from the article best describes Elizabeth Eckford?

☐ a. "Suddenly she wasn't sure she could make it."

☐ b. "Walking toward the school, Elizabeth felt her knees start to shake."

☐ c. "She didn't want the crowd to know she was scared."

3. From the statements below, choose those that you believe the author would agree with.

☐ a. By the end of the school year, most of the white high school students admired the black students.

☐ b. The black students were frightened by their first-year experiences at Central High.

☐ c. The white students' hatred of the Little Rock Nine was largely a result of ignorance and fear.

4. What does the author imply by saying "They were finally safe from the throngs of angry adults, but they still had to face the scorn and hatred of their fellow students"?

☐ a. The Little Rock Nine were safe once they entered the high school.

☐ b. The white students in Central High were as prejudiced as their parents.

☐ c. The white students in the school were angrier and more vicious in their attacks than the adults had been.

_____ Number of correct answers

Record your personal assessment of your work on the Critical Thinking Chart on page 136.

Summarizing and Paraphrasing

Put an X in the box next to the correct answer.

1. Below are summaries of the article. Choose the summary that says all the most important things about the article but in the fewest words.

☐ a. Nine black students endured threats, humiliation, and physical abuse in order to attend an all-white school in Little Rock, Arkansas.

☐ b. White adults and students tried to prevent nine black students, known as the Little Rock Nine, from attending an all-white school in Little Rock, Arkansas.

☐ c. President Eisenhower ordered the National Guard and army paratroopers to protect the Little Rock Nine.

2. Choose the sentence that correctly restates the following sentence from the article:

"At the end of the school year, the black students emerged from Central High exhausted but victorious."

☐ a. The black students were glad that their year of torment was over.

☐ b. At the end of the year, the black students were tired, but they had won several school awards.

☐ c. After a year in the school, the black students were tired from their ordeal but very pleased with their achievement.

_____ Number of correct answers

Record your personal assessment of your work on the Critical Thinking Chart on page 136.

Critical Thinking

Put an X in the box next to the correct answer for questions 1 and 4. Follow the directions provided for the other questions.

1. Based on the information in paragraph 15, you can predict that

☐ a. no one would torment the black high school students during the following year.

☐ b. more and more black students would begin integrating all-white schools throughout the United States.

☐ c. the white students would formally apologize to the black students.

2. Choose from the letters below to correctly complete the following statement. Write the letters on the lines.

On the positive side, _____, but on the negative side _____.

a. the black teenagers suffered a great deal of humiliation

b. President Dwight Eisenhower called out the National Guard

c. the Little Rock Nine paved the way for other blacks

3. Read paragraph 11. Then choose from the letters below to correctly complete the following statement. Write the letters on the lines.

According to paragraph 11, _____ because _____ .

a. President Eisenhower forced Governor Faubus to step down

b. the nine black teenagers attended Central High

c. President Eisenhower sent in army paratroopers to accompany the black students to their classes

4. How are the nine black teenagers examples of heroes?

☐ a. The students continued to attend Central High, in spite of their cruel treatment.

☐ b. The students' behavior inspired the white Central High students to accept racial integration.

☐ c. The black students helped put an end to racial discrimination in Little Rock.

5. Which paragraphs from the article provide evidence that supports your answer to question 2?

_____

_____ Number of correct answers

Record your personal assessment of your work on the Critical Thinking Chart on page 136.

Personal Response

I know how Minnejean Brown feels because

_____

_____

_____

_____

Self-Assessment

When reading the article, I was having trouble with

_____

_____

_____

_____

CHRISTOPHER REEVE
A Real Superman

In his movie roles as Superman, Christopher Reeve played a hero based on a comic-book character. Today, Reeve plays a real-life hero.

He was "faster than a speeding bullet, more powerful than a locomotive, able to leap tall buildings in a single bound." He was Superman—the world's greatest superhero. When Christopher Reeve was picked to play this role in films in 1977, audiences across the country cheered with approval. Like Superman, Christopher was dashing, handsome, and strong. Like Superman, he seemed nearly invincible. He skied, sailed, flew planes, went scuba diving, rode horses, played tennis—and did it all with skill and ease. No one could imagine Christopher Reeve any other way.

2   All that changed on May 27, 1995. Christopher was in Virginia with his wife, Dana Morosini, and their young son Will. He had entered a three-day horse riding competition there. His horse, a seven-year-old thoroughbred named Eastern Express, appeared to be in fine shape. The 42-year-old Christopher looked equally fit and relaxed. As always, he wore his protective vest and his riding helmet during the competition.

3   The competition was going well for Christopher. He wasn't in first place, but he wasn't in last, either. His score was somewhere in the middle—good enough so that he was "pretty excited about it," according to horse trainer Lisa Reid. Reid watched Christopher as he began a two-mile jumping event. The course included 15 obstacles. Together, Christopher and Eastern Express flew easily over the first two obstacles. The third one should have been no problem, either. It consisted of a three-foot-high zigzagging rail fence. As Christopher himself said, it was "one of the easiest jumps" on the course.

4   "The horse was coming into the fence beautifully," Lisa Reid later reported. "The rhythm was fine and Chris was fine, and they were going at a good pace."

5   What happened next was a freak accident. Somehow communication between horse and rider broke down. Without warning, Eastern Express stopped short. Christopher, however, kept going. He pitched forward over the horse's head. Ordinarily, he could have used his hands to break his fall. In that case, the accident might not have been bad; Christopher might have ended up with nothing more than a sprained wrist and a few bruised muscles.

6   But Christopher's hands got caught in the reins. He couldn't get them free, and so he had no way to lessen the impact of the fall. He landed on his head with sickening force and then just lay there—unconscious, not moving, not even breathing. As one witness recalled, it looked as though "the life had gone out of him."

7   Medical workers managed to keep Christopher alive as they rushed him to the local hospital. From there, they sent him by helicopter to the University of Virginia Medical Center. No one knew how long he would survive. His wife was told to say good-bye to him.

8   For several days, Christopher's life hung in the balance. On the fourth day, when he finally opened his eyes, he found himself surrounded by tubes and machines. His entire body was in traction. His head was immobilized, and his lungs were hooked up to a respirator.

9   That was when Christopher learned the extent of his injuries. He had broken his spinal cord near the base of his skull, resulting in paralysis from the neck down. He could not speak. He could not even breathe on his own. Doctors needed to operate to stabilize his condition, but they hadn't been able to do so. Pneumonia had set in, making surgery too risky. At that point, doctors gave him only a 50-50 chance of surviving.

10   Despair filled Christopher Reeve's heart. He thought perhaps it would be best if he simply gave up. Dying seemed like the easiest and least painful thing to do. He thought it might be best for his

Christopher Reeve (with Bryant Gumble) at the 1997 Emmy Awards ceremony

family, too. Then he saw his wife Dana standing next to him, saying, "You're still you, and I love you."

11   From that moment on, Christopher thought only about living. Gathering his courage, he began to fight for his life. A few days later, the pneumonia cleared up and Christopher underwent the operation. That helped restore some feeling to his upper body. Still, doctors emphasized his limitations. He would never walk again. He would probably never even breathe again without the aid of the respirator.

12   Christopher set out to prove the doctors wrong. First of all, he wanted to breathe on his own. Five months after the accident, he asked to be taken off the respirator. He managed just 10 feeble breaths before being reconnected to the breathing tube.

13   Refusing to be discouraged, Christopher took a few more breaths the next day. By the fourth day, he was able to breathe seven minutes without assistance. The doctors were both surprised and impressed. From there, Christopher rapidly increased his endurance. After three months, he could sustain himself for 90 minutes at a time. He still needed the respirator when he spoke; nevertheless, he was delighted with his progress. Christopher also managed to wean

himself off his feeding tube. By the end of 1995, he was able to go home.

14   Soon after that, Christopher felt ready to face the world again. He had a message to spread. He wanted to tell people that no matter what challenges they faced, they shouldn't give up. Christopher began to make public appearances. He gave a motivational speech in Toronto. He spoke at a Boston University graduation. He even showed up at the 1996 Academy Awards ceremony. Wherever Christopher appeared, his speeches met with standing ovations—and many teary faces.

15   Christopher also went back to work. Clearly he couldn't play the roles he'd played in the past. Instead, he turned to directing. His first film, *In the Gloaming*, proved he had not lost his creative spark.

16   Meanwhile, Christopher urged researchers to continue looking for ways to fix spinal cord injuries. He helped set up a new center devoted to spinal cord research. All the while, he held fast to a positive attitude, saying, "I totally believe that within a decade, I'm going to be up and walking again."

17   Despite his brave attitude, Christopher has had his share of "down" times. In the year following his accident, he had problems with blood clots. Later he got pneumonia again. One day while doing

physical therapy, he fell to the floor and broke his arm.

18   Every day he struggled with the reality of his condition. "In the morning, I need 20 minutes to cry," he told a reporter. After nighttime dreams of running and playing with his son, he needed the 20 minutes "to wake up and make that shift...to really allow yourself the feeling of loss...."

19   But after the tears, Christopher always whispered, "And now, forward!" With those words, Christopher Reeve proved that although he had lost control of his body, he still had his courage, his spirit, and his inner strength. In that sense, he still was—and always would be—Superman. ✿

If you have been timed while reading this article, enter your reading time below. Then turn to the Words-per-Minute Table on page 133 and look up your reading speed (words per minute). Enter your reading speed on the graph on page 134.

Reading Time: Lesson 14

_____ : _____

Minutes   Seconds

A | Finding the Main Idea

One statement below expresses the main idea of the article. One statement is too general, or too broad. The other statement explains only part of the article; it is too narrow. Label the statements using the following key:

M—Main Idea   **B—Too Broad**   **N—Too Narrow**

_____ 1. Christopher Reeve became paralyzed from the neck down as a result of a horseback-riding accident.

_____ 2. Christopher Reeve has shown superhero courage in dealing with his injury.

_____ 3. After becoming paralyzed from the neck down, Christopher Reeve has fought courageously to overcome his injuries.

_____ Score 15 points for a correct M answer.

_____ Score 5 points for each correct B or N answer.

_____ **Total Score:** Finding the Main Idea

B | Recalling Facts

How well do you remember the facts in the article? Put an X in the box next to the answer that correctly completes each statement about the article.

1. Christopher's fall was particularly bad because
   ☐ a. he wasn't wearing a helmet at the time.
   ☐ b. his hands got caught in the reins.
   ☐ c. he landed on his back.

2. After the accident, doctors said that
   ☐ a. Christopher had a 50-50 chance of surviving.
   ☐ b. it would be best if Christopher simply gave up.
   ☐ c. there was nothing they could do for Christopher.

3. Five months after the accident, Christopher
   ☐ a. tried to take a few steps.
   ☐ b. was able to go home.
   ☐ c. tried to breathe without a respirator.

4. In 1996, Christopher Reeve
   ☐ a. appeared in a movie called *In the Gloaming*.
   ☐ b. made a guest appearance at the Academy Awards ceremony.
   ☐ c. began researching ways to fix spinal cord injuries.

5. While doing physical therapy a year after his injury, Christopher
   ☐ a. developed pneumonia.
   ☐ b. cried for 20 minutes.
   ☐ c. fell and broke his arm.

Score 5 points for each correct answer.

_____ **Total Score:** Recalling Facts

C | Making Inferences

When you combine your own experience and information from a text to draw a conclusion that is not directly stated in that text, you are making an inference. Below are five statements that may or may not be inferences based on information in the article. Label the statements using the following key:

C—Correct Inference   F—Faulty Inference

_____ 1. One day Christopher Reeve will play Superman in the movies again.

_____ 2. Christopher Reeve was not an experienced horseback rider.

_____ 3. Christopher does not allow self-pity to distract him from his goals.

_____ 4. When Christopher Reeve appears in public, he has a powerful impact on his audience.

_____ 5. The doctors who emphasized Christopher's limitations and told him that he would probably never breathe on his own were incompetent.

Score 5 points for each correct answer.

_____ **Total Score:** Making Inferences

D | Using Words Precisely

Each numbered sentence below contains an underlined word or phrase from the article. Following the sentence are three definitions. One definition is closest to the meaning of the underlined word. One definition is opposite or nearly opposite. Label those two definitions using the following key. Do not label the remaining definition.

C—Closest   O—Opposite or Nearly Opposite

1. Like Superman, he seemed nearly <u>invincible</u>.

_____ a. handsome

_____ b. weak

_____ c. indestructible

2. He couldn't get them free, and so he had no way to <u>lessen</u> the impact of the fall.

_____ a. increase

_____ b. reduce

_____ c. avoid

3. Pneumonia had set in, making surgery too <u>risky</u>.

_____ a. safe

_____ b. necessary

_____ c. hazardous

4. Christopher also managed to <u>wean</u> himself off his feeding tube.

_____ a. become addicted to

_____ b. gradually phase out

_____ c. attach by oneself

5. Wherever Christopher appeared, his speeches met with <u>standing ovations</u>—and many teary faces.

_____ a. a moment of silent prayer

_____ b. silent disapproval

_____ c. thunderous applause

_____ Score 3 points for each correct C answer.

_____ Score 2 points for each correct O answer.

_____ **Total Score:** Using Words Precisely

Enter the four total scores in the spaces below, and add them together to find your Reading Comprehension Score. Then record your score on the graph on page 135.

Score	Question Type	Lesson 14
_____	Finding the Main Idea	
_____	Recalling Facts	
_____	Making Inferences	
_____	Using Words Precisely	
_____	**Reading Comprehension Score**	

Author's Approach

Put an X in the box next to the correct answer.

1. The author uses the first sentence of the article to

☐ a. inform the reader about Superman.

☐ b. describe the qualities of a well-known hero.

☐ c. compare Christopher Reeve and Superman.

2. What does the author mean by the statement, "In that sense, he still was—and always would be—Superman"?

☐ a. Superman and Christopher Reeve still had many things in common.

☐ b. Audiences would always remember Reeve as Superman.

☐ c. Reeve's bravery and determination proved he would always have the qualities of a superhero.

3. What is the author's purpose in writing "Christopher Reeve: A Real Superman"?

☐ a. To encourage the reader to be courageous and think positively

☐ b. To inform the reader about the dangers of horse riding competitions

☐ c. To describe a situation in which heroism is defined by inner strength and courage

4. Which of the following statements from the article best describes Christopher Reeve?

☐ a. "Every day he struggled with the reality of his condition."

☐ b. "He skied, sailed, flew planes, went scuba diving, rode horses, played tennis—and did it all with skill and ease."

☐ c. "Gathering his courage, he began to fight for his life."

_____ Number of correct answers

Record your personal assessment of your work on the Critical Thinking Chart on page 136.

Summarizing and Paraphrasing

Put an X in the box next to the correct answer for questions 2 and 3. Follow the directions provided for the other question.

1. Complete the following one-sentence summary of the article using the lettered phrases from the phrase bank below. Write the letters on the lines.

> **Phrase Bank:**
> a. a life-threatening accident
> b. Reeve inspiring others with his courage
> c. Reeve's struggle against his paralysis

The article about Christopher Reeve begins with _____, goes on to explain _____, and ends with _____.

2. Read the following statement about the article. Then read the paraphrase of that statement. Choose the reason that best tells why the paraphrase does not say the same thing as the statement.

Statement: Christopher Reeve was heroic in his efforts to battle his spinal cord injuries. His courage and inner strength helped him fight for his life and ultimately improve his condition.

Paraphrase: A man overcame his injuries. He worked hard to improve his condition; therefore, he is a hero.

☐ a. Paraphrase says too much.

☐ b. Paraphrase doesn't say enough.

☐ c. Paraphrase doesn't agree with the statement about the article.

3. Choose the letter that correctly restates the following sentence from the article:

"As one witness recalled, it looked as though 'the life had gone out of him.'"

☐ a. One person who saw the accident remembered that Christopher Reeve seemed lifeless and empty.

☐ b. A witness recalled that Christopher Reeve was no longer happy and cheerful.

☐ c. A friend remembered saying, "The life he once had was gone."

_____ Number of correct answers

Record your personal assessment of your work on the Critical Thinking Chart on page 136.

Critical Thinking

Put an X in the box next to the correct answer for questions 1, 3, and 4. Follow the directions provided for the other question.

1. Based on what the article told about Christopher Reeve, you can predict that

☐ a. he will star in another Superman movie.

☐ b. he will visit his horse, Eastern Express, and ride again.

☐ c. Christopher will direct other movies and begin a fund for spinal cord research.

2. Using what you know about Superman and what is told about Christopher Reeve in the article, name three ways Reeve is similar to and three ways he is different from the Superman hero. Cite the paragraph number(s) where you found details in the article to support your conclusions.

Similarities

_____

_____

_____

Differences

_____

_____

_____

3. What was the effect of Reeve's wife saying, "You're still you, and I love you"?

☐ a. Reeve knew he could not give up and had to keep living.

☐ b. He understood he was still the same person he was before the accident.

☐ c. He knew his injuries weren't serious.

4. What did you have to do to answer question 3?

☐ a. find a cause (why something happened)

☐ b. find an effect (something that happened)

☐ c. draw a conclusion (a sensible statement based on the text and your experience)

_____ Number of correct answers

Record your personal assessment of your work on the Critical Thinking Chart on page 136.

Personal Response

This article is different from other stories about heroes I've read because

_____

and Christopher Reeve is unlike other heroes because

_____

_____

_____

Self-Assessment

A word or phrase in the article that I do not understand is

_____

_____

CRITICAL THINKING

Compare and Contrast

Think about the articles you have read in Unit Two. Pick the four heroes or groups of heroes you most enjoyed reading about or you most admired. Write their names in the first column of the chart below. Use information you learned from the articles to fill in the empty boxes in the chart.

My Hero	How did he, she, or they affect other people's lives?	What was the greatest difficulty this hero overcame?	What did other people think of these heroic actions at the time?

Suppose you were interviewing one of the heroes or groups you read about in this unit. Write three questions you would ask in your interview.

_____

_____

_____

Words-per-Minute Table

Unit Two

Directions: If you were timed while reading an article, refer to the Reading Time you recorded in the box at the end of the article. Use this words-per-minute table to determine your reading speed for that article. Then plot your reading speed on the graph on page 134.

Lesson No. of Words	8 1366	9 1082	10 1437	11 1332	12 1384	13 1160	14 1150	Seconds
1:30	911	721	958	888	923	773	767	90
1:40	820	649	862	799	830	696	690	100
1:50	745	590	784	727	755	633	627	110
2:00	683	541	719	666	692	580	575	120
2:10	630	499	663	615	639	535	531	130
2:20	585	464	616	571	593	497	493	140
2:30	546	433	575	533	554	464	460	150
2:40	512	406	539	500	519	435	431	160
2:50	482	382	507	470	488	409	406	170
3:00	455	361	479	444	461	387	383	180
3:10	431	342	454	421	437	366	363	190
3:20	410	325	431	400	415	348	345	200
3:30	390	309	411	381	395	331	329	210
3:40	373	295	392	363	377	316	314	220
3:50	356	282	375	347	361	303	300	230
4:00	342	271	359	333	346	290	288	240
4:10	328	260	345	320	332	278	276	250
4:20	315	250	332	307	319	268	265	260
4:30	304	240	319	296	308	258	256	270
4:40	293	232	308	285	297	249	246	280
4:50	283	224	297	276	286	240	238	290
5:00	273	216	287	266	277	232	230	300
5:10	264	209	278	258	268	225	223	310
5:20	256	203	269	250	260	218	216	320
5:30	248	197	261	242	252	211	209	330
5:40	241	191	254	235	244	205	203	340
5:50	234	185	246	228	237	199	197	350
6:00	228	180	240	222	231	193	192	360
6:10	222	175	233	216	224	188	186	370
6:20	216	171	227	210	219	183	182	380
6:30	210	166	221	205	213	178	177	390
6:40	205	162	216	200	208	174	173	400
6:50	200	158	210	195	203	170	168	410
7:00	195	155	205	190	198	166	164	420
7:10	191	151	200	186	193	162	160	430
7:20	186	148	196	182	189	158	157	440
7:30	182	144	192	178	184	155	153	450
7:40	178	141	187	174	181	151	150	460
7:50	174	138	183	170	177	148	147	470
8:00	171	135	180	167	173	145	144	480

Minutes and Seconds

Plotting Your Progress: Reading Speed

Unit Two

Directions: If you were timed while reading an article, write your words-per-minute rate for that in the box under the number of the lesson. Then plot your reading speed on the graph by putting a small X on the line directly above the number of the lesson, across from the number of words per minute you read. As you mark your speed for each lesson, graph your progress by drawing a line to connect the X's.

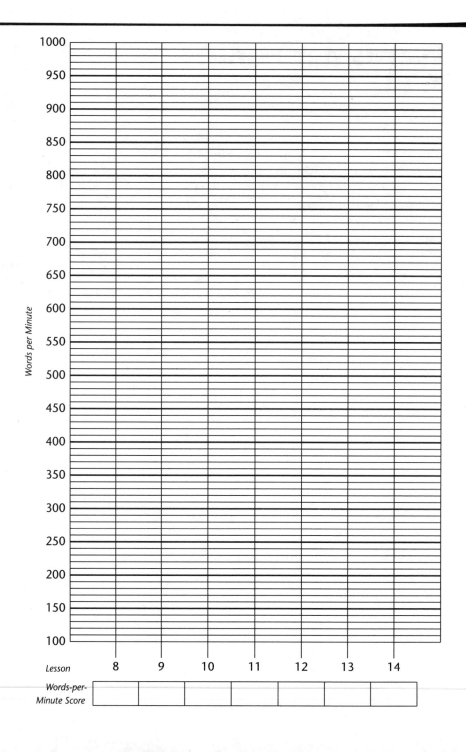

Lesson	8	9	10	11	12	13	14
Words-per-Minute Score							

Plotting Your Progress: Reading Comprehension

Unit Two

Directions: Write your Reading Comprehension score for each lesson in the box under the number of the lesson. Then plot your score on the graph by putting a small X on the line directly above the number of the lesson and across from the score you earned. As you mark your score for each lesson, graph your progress by drawing a line to connect the X's.

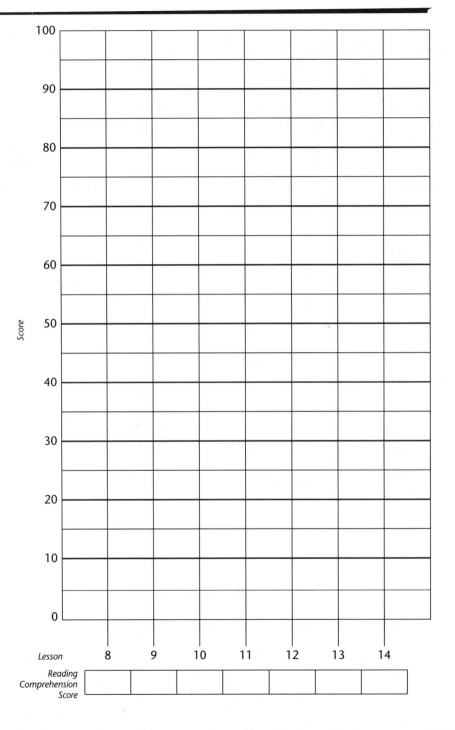

Score

Lesson   8   9   10   11   12   13   14

Reading Comprehension Score

Plotting Your Progress: Critical Thinking

Unit Two

Directions: Work with your teacher to evaluate your responses to the Critical Thinking questions for each lesson. Then fill in the appropriate spaces in the chart below. For each lesson and each type of Critical Thinking question, do the following: Mark a minus sign (–) in the box to indicate areas in which you feel you could improve. Mark a plus sign (+) to indicate areas in which you feel you did well. Mark a minus-slash-plus sign (–/+) to indicate areas in which you had mixed success. Then write any comments you have about your performance, including ideas for improvement.

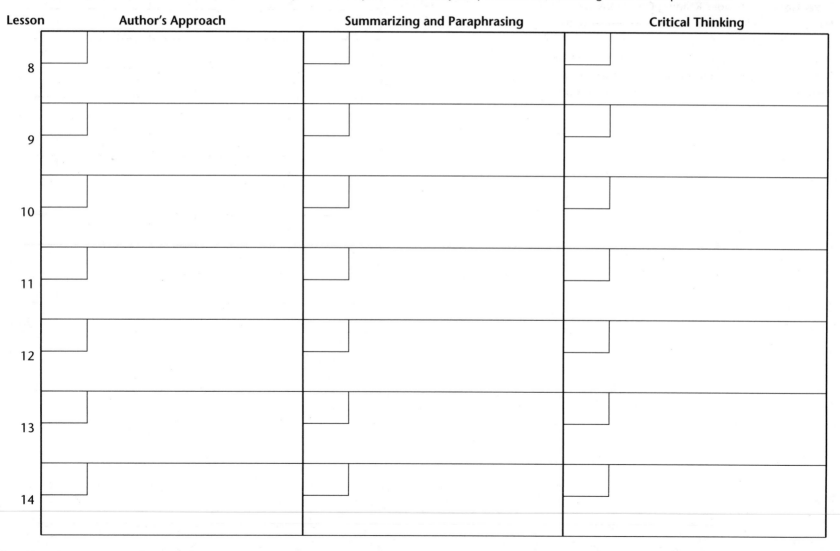

Lesson	Author's Approach	Summarizing and Paraphrasing	Critical Thinking
8			
9			
10			
11			
12			
13			
14			

UNIT THREE

LARRY CHAMPAGNE
Aboard a Runaway Bus

The day started quietly enough for 10-year-old Larry Champagne III. He and his little brother, Jerrick, said good-bye to their mom and walked out the door of their home in St. Louis, Missouri. As usual, they boarded the school bus bound for Bellerive Elementary School at about 7:25 A.M. They had no way of knowing that before they reached Bellerive, their lives—and the lives of the other 18 students on the bus—would be in jeopardy.

2 The ride to school was a long one, so Larry settled back in his seat. He had plenty to occupy his thoughts. Three weeks earlier, his father had been stabbed to death on the street outside his apartment. Although Larry's parents had been divorced for several years, Larry had remained close to his dad and had taken the news of his death hard. The principal at Bellerive knew about the tragedy, but Larry hadn't told many of his classmates. He found it too painful to talk about.

3 On this morning, October 3, 1995, bus driver Ernestine Blackman maneuvered the bus out onto U.S. Highway 40. By now it was almost 8:00; the westbound lanes were crowded with rush-hour traffic. Blackman speeded up to about 55 miles per hour to keep up with the flow of traffic. Suddenly, Larry and the other children felt the bus swerve. Looking up, they saw Blackman collapse, falling completely out of her seat and landing on the bus's stairwell. No one knew it at the time, but the 42-year-old driver had just suffered a major stroke.

4 With their driver lying incapacitated on the floor, the children knew they were in trouble. The bus, now totally out of control, careened across three lanes of traffic and banged against the guardrails on the side of the highway. Larry later described it this way: "The bus started swaying side to side and hit the guardrail twice. That made everyone fall and hit the window. I thought we were going to crash." In fact, Larry said, "I thought we were going to die."

5 Larry was not alone in this assessment. To those who witnessed the scene, the death of the children on the bus seemed almost a certainty. Many of the young passengers began to cry. Outside, drivers who saw the runaway bus honked their horns and swerved out of the way, but there was nothing they could do to save the children trapped inside.

6 Then, all of a sudden, Larry Champagne jumped out of his seat. He ran down the aisle and slid into the driver's seat. At that moment, he was not thinking about his own problems. He was not focused on the sadness and depression he felt over the death of his father. Instead, Larry concentrated on

Larry Champagne III sits on a school bus like the one he brought under control on a busy St. Louis highway on October 3, 1995.

Larry Champagne III on his front steps

remembering what his grandfather had taught him about motor vehicles.

7   Larry and his grandfather, Larry Champagne Sr., had often spent time together fixing up an old Chevy pickup truck. As they worked, Mr. Champagne had given Larry some instructions on how to operate a vehicle. Thanks to those sessions, Larry knew what to do. He grabbed the steering wheel with his hands while his foot felt around for the brake. When he located it, he stomped down on it hard.

8   As the air brakes squealed, Larry called to three of his friends, Angelo and Gregory Knight and Imani Butler. He wanted them to come help the bus driver, who still lay crumpled on the floor. The three friends nervously rose from their seats and made their way down the aisle to the front of the bus. They tried to rouse Blackman but were unable to get a response. The children, aged 9 to 11, were not strong enough to move her.

9   Meanwhile, other drivers were trying to keep from hitting the erratically moving bus. Most managed to avoid a collision, but one pickup truck plowed into the back of the bus. The impact knocked Angelo and Imani off balance. Both were injured, although neither was seriously hurt.

10   Moments later Larry managed to bring the bus to a complete halt. The children could barely believe it; they were all still alive! They weren't completely out of danger yet, though; they were still stranded on the bus in the middle of a busy highway. One vehicle had already hit them, and others might soon follow. Luckily, a passerby with a cellular phone called the police. Also, Crystal Wright, one of the children on the bus, handed Blackman's radio microphone to someone outside who then radioed the bus company's headquarters.

11   Within minutes, authorities arrived on the scene. Ernestine Blackman was rushed to a nearby hospital, where she was listed in serious condition. Five children who had sustained minor injuries were also taken to local hospitals for examination. The other 15 children, including Larry Champagne, were put on another bus and transported the rest of the way to Bellerive Elementary School.

12   When the children finally arrived at their school, many of them were still shaking from their close call. They were grateful to be alive and unharmed. And they knew whom they had to thank for that. Larry Champagne's courage and quick thinking had brought them through the morning's events unscathed. Gregory Knight remembered, "When we got off, everybody said, 'Thank you, Larry, for saving our lives.'" Some of the children ran up to Principal Ken Russell chanting, "Larry saved our lives, Larry saved our lives."

13   Larry himself was modest about his role in the rescue. To a reporter, he simply said, "My grandmother always tells me to be confident and to do what's right." To his school principal, Larry opened up a little more. He explained what perhaps made him feel best about his actions. "I think my dad would be proud of me," he said.

If you have been timed while reading this article, enter your reading time below. Then turn to the Words-per-Minute Table on page 195 and look up your reading speed (words per minute). Enter your reading speed on the graph on page 196.

Reading Time: Lesson 15

_____ : _____
Minutes   Seconds

A | Finding the Main Idea

One statement below expresses the main idea of the article. One statement is too general, or too broad. The other statement explains only part of the article; it is too narrow. Label the statements using the following key:

M—Main Idea   **B—Too Broad**   **N—Too Narrow**

_____ 1. After his school bus driver collapsed, Larry Champagne managed to stop the bus and save the lives of its young passengers.

_____ 2. Larry Champagne's grandfather taught him how to operate motor vehicles.

_____ 3. Larry Champagne's quick thinking in a crisis saved his life and the lives of the other children.

_____ Score 15 points for a correct M answer.

_____ Score 5 points for each correct B or N answer.

_____ **Total Score:** Finding the Main Idea

B | Recalling Facts

How well do you remember the facts in the article? Put an X in the box next to the answer that correctly completes each statement about the article.

1. When the bus ride began, Larry was thinking about his
   - ☐ a. grandfather.
   - ☐ b. mother.
   - ☐ c. father.

2. The school bus suddenly swerved out of control because the
   - ☐ a. bus had been hit by a pickup truck.
   - ☐ b. driver had suffered a major stroke.
   - ☐ c. bus hit the guardrails on the side of the highway.

3. Larry jumped into the driver's seat and
   - ☐ a. called the police on a cellular phone.
   - ☐ b. tried to revive Ernestine Blackman.
   - ☐ c. stomped hard on the brake.

4. The child who handed Blackman's radio microphone to someone outside the bus was
   - ☐ a. Crystal Wright.
   - ☐ b. Gregory Knight.
   - ☐ c. Imani Butler.

5. When the children got off the bus, they all
   - ☐ a. thanked Larry.
   - ☐ b. talked to a reporter.
   - ☐ c. talked to their principal.

_____ Score 5 points for each correct answer.

_____ **Total Score:** Recalling Facts

C | Making Inferences

When you combine your own experience and information from a text to draw a conclusion that is not directly stated in that text, you are making an inference. Below are five statements that may or may not be inferences based on information in the article. Label the statements using the following key:

C—Correct Inference   F—Faulty Inference

_____ 1. Larry Champagne could take over the bus driver's job.

_____ 2. Larry doesn't panic in a crisis.

_____ 3. Most of the children on the bus would have been seriously injured if no one had stopped the bus.

_____ 4. Larry's grandparents play an important role in his life.

_____ 5. The other children resented the attention Larry received from the reporter and the principal.

Score 5 points for each correct answer.

_____ **Total Score:** Making Inferences

D | Using Words Precisely

Each numbered sentence below contains an underlined word or phrase from the article. Following the sentence are three definitions. One definition is closest to the meaning of the underlined word. One definition is opposite or nearly opposite. Label those two definitions using the following key. Do not label the remaining definition.

C—Closest   O—Opposite or Nearly Opposite

1. They had no way of knowing that before they reached Bellerive, their lives—and the lives of the other 18 students on the bus—would be <u>in jeopardy</u>.

   _____ a. famous

   _____ b. in danger

   _____ c. safe and secure

2. On this morning, October 3, 1995, bus driver Ernestine Blackman <u>maneuvered</u> the bus out onto U.S. Highway 40.

   _____ a. guided skillfully

   _____ b. lost control

   _____ c. suddenly stopped

3. Suddenly, Larry and the other children felt the bus <u>swerve</u>.

   _____ a. shake

   _____ b. make a sudden change in direction

   _____ c. continue along a straight line

4. With their driver lying <u>incapacitated</u> on the floor, the children knew they were in trouble.

_____ a. powerless

_____ b. dead

_____ c. energetic

5. Larry Champagne's courage and quick thinking had brought them through the morning's events <u>unscathed</u>.

_____ a. injured

_____ b. not frightened

_____ c. unharmed

_____ Score 3 points for each correct C answer.

_____ Score 2 points for each correct O answer.

_____ **Total Score:** Using Words Precisely

Enter the four total scores in the spaces below, and add them together to find your Reading Comprehension Score. Then record your score on the graph on page 197.

Score	Question Type	Lesson 15
_____	Finding the Main Idea	
_____	Recalling Facts	
_____	Making Inferences	
_____	Using Words Precisely	
_____	**Reading Comprehension Score**	

Author's Approach

Put an X in the box next to the correct answer.

1. The main purpose of the first paragraph is to

☐ a. convey an atmosphere of suspense.

☐ b. inform the reader about Larry and Jerrick Champagne.

☐ c. compare Larry and Jerrick Champagne.

2. Which of the following statements from the article best describes Larry Champagne III?

☐ a. "Larry and his grandfather, Larry Champagne Sr., had often spent time together fixing up an old Chevy pickup truck."

☐ b. "Although Larry's parents had been divorced for several years, Larry had remained close to his dad and had taken the news of his death hard."

☐ c. "Larry himself was modest about his role in the rescue."

3. In this article, "When the children finally arrived at their school, many of them were still shaking from their close call" means

☐ a. the children were still badly frightened by their experience on the runaway bus.

☐ b. all of the children were anxious to telephone their parents and tell them what happened.

☐ c. when the children arrived at the school, they shook hands with their friends and told them what had happened.

4. The author probably wrote this article in order to

☐ a. tell young readers how to operate motor vehicles in an emergency.

☐ b. describe a young boy's bravery and quick thinking during a crisis.

☐ c. entertain the reader with an exciting story.

_____ Number of correct answers

Record your personal assessment of your work on the Critical Thinking Chart on page 198.

Summarizing and Paraphrasing

Put an X in the box next to the correct answer for question 3. Follow the directions provided for the other questions.

1. Look for the important ideas and events in paragraphs 6 and 7. Summarize those paragraphs in one or two sentences.

_____

_____

_____

2. Complete the following one-sentence summary of the article using the lettered phrases from the phrase bank below. Write the letters on the lines.

> **Phrase Bank:**
> a. the collapse of his school bus driver
> b. the safe arrival of the school children at their school
> c. Larry's efforts to stop the bus

The article about Larry Champagne III begins with _____, goes on to explain _____, and ends with _____.

3. Choose the best one-sentence paraphrase for the following sentence from the article:

"He was not focused on the sadness and depression he felt over the death of his father."

☐ a. Larry no longer felt saddened by his father's death.

☐ b. Larry stopped concentrating on his sadness over his father's death.

☐ c. Larry was overcome with sadness because he could not stop thinking about his father.

> _____ Number of correct answers
>
> Record your personal assessment of your work on the Critical Thinking Chart on page 198.

Critical Thinking

Put an X in the box next to the correct answer for questions 1 and 3. Follow the directions provided for the other questions.

1. Based on the events in the article, you can predict that the following will happen next:

☐ a. Larry Champagne would stop taking the school bus to school.

☐ b. Larry Champagne would be treated like a hero in his school and community.

☐ c. Larry Champagne would brag so much about his heroism on the school bus that he would lose his friends.

2. Choose from the letters below to correctly complete the following statement. Write the letters on the lines.

On the positive side, _____, but on the negative side _____.

a. Larry Champagne thought that his father would be proud of him

b. several children were injured during the incident

c. his father was dead

3. What was the effect of Ernestine Blackman's collapse?

☐ a. She suffered a major stroke.

☐ b. The lanes of the highway were crowded with traffic.

☐ c. The bus swerved out of control down the highway.

4. In which paragraph did you find the information or details to answer question 3?

_____

_____ Number of correct answers

Record your personal assessment of your work on the Critical Thinking Chart on page 198.

Personal Response

How do you think Larry Champagne felt when he slid into the bus driver's seat?

_____

_____

_____

Self-Assessment

What concepts or ideas from the article were difficult?

_____

_____

_____

Which were easy?

_____

_____

FRANK SERPICO
An Honest Cop

New York City Detective Frank Serpico testifies on corruption in the New York City Police Department before the Knapp Commission in 1972.

Police officer Frank Serpico lay in the Brooklyn Jewish Hospital in critical condition. Four days earlier, on February 3, 1971, he had been shot in the head while trying to arrest a heroin dealer. Luckily the bullet had not reached Serpico's brain. But it had torn through his facial muscles, crashed through his left sinus and hit his jawbone. His face was swollen to twice its normal size, and a bloody fluid oozed from his ear. The doctors were not yet sure if he would live.

2 As he lay conscious but heavily sedated, a nurse brought him an envelope. Inside was a greeting card bearing the printed message "Recuperate Quickly." But the person who sent the card had crossed out the word *Recuperate* and had written in the word *Die*.

3 Although the card was not signed, Serpico was sure it was from a fellow cop. Only a member of the New York Police Department would have sent such a vicious message. Serpico knew that most of the men and women in the department hated him, or at least mistrusted him. He had broken the number one rule of the force. He had exposed the corruption of

his fellow officers. In their view, Frank Serpico had squealed.

4   When Serpico became a police officer in early 1960, he just wanted to be a good, honest cop. He soon learned that that wasn't so easy. Almost immediately, he discovered that most of the officers on the force did not share his lofty vision of police work. To Serpico, being a cop meant upholding the law, protecting honest citizens from outlaws, and setting a good example for society. To most of his coworkers in the 81st Precinct, however, being a cop simply meant having a good, steady job with the opportunity to make lots of money.

5   In his early days on the force, Serpico was amazed by what he saw. He found that many cops beat their suspects. Others slept on the job or demanded free meals from local restaurants in return for special favors. Worst of all, most of the officers in the precinct accepted bribes. At first the bribes that Serpico learned about were small—$30 or so for letting someone get away with a traffic violation. But when Serpico moved up into the plainclothes division, he saw that the problem of graft was a lot bigger than that.

6   While working as an undercover cop, Serpico discovered that virtually all plainclothes officers were corrupt. Almost all of them accepted many thousands of dollars in bribes each year. The bribes came from people who were operating illegal gambling rackets. In return for the money, cops allowed the gamblers to continue their illegal activities. Those few officers who weren't taking money simply looked the other way while their partners got richer and richer.

7   At first Frank just looked the other way too. Time after time, he refused to take the payoffs that were offered to him. Gradually, however, he began to feel that he needed to do something more. He couldn't continue to stand by and watch while hundreds of dishonest police officers worked out illegal deals with gamblers. Still, he wasn't sure what to do. The more he thought about it, the more convinced he became that many of his superior officers were also accepting bribes.

8   Serpico pondered the situation for months. Then, in July of 1966, something happened that forced him into action. A uniformed cop handed him an envelope, telling him it was from the ringleader of a gambling circle in the district. When Serpico opened the envelope, he found that it contained $300 in small bills. It was then that he knew he could not ignore the problem any longer. He had to report the incident to the authorities. But who could he trust? How could he know which of his superior officers were honest and which weren't? How could he make sure that his charges would lead to an investigation and not to a cover-up?

9   There were no clear answers to any of those questions, but Serpico knew he had to tell someone what was going on. He began to contact high-ranking police

Frank Serpico upon graduation from the New York Police Academy, 1960

officers outside his precinct. He talked to one after another, but no one seemed willing to do anything. Some were too scared, some were too lazy, and some were probably guilty of illegal activities themselves. In any event, Frank Serpico kept trying. He went to division captains, to the deputy chief inspector, to the commissioner of investigation, and to one of the mayor's closest advisors in city hall. He even sent messages to the police commissioner's first deputy, who was in charge of all police matters. Still nothing happened.

10   Meanwhile, the cops on the force began to get suspicious of Serpico. They resented the fact that he didn't take bribes. They began to worry that he was going to squeal on them. Soon, only a few of the plainclothes officers in his division would talk to him.

11   Finally, after fighting with top officials for a year and a half, Serpico got some results. A small investigation was made into his allegations of graft and corruption. But because the investigation was handled poorly, it turned up only enough evidence to arrest eight plainclothes cops. No higher-ranking officers were charged, and nothing was done to restructure the system.

12   Still, word spread quickly through the entire police department that Serpico had squealed. After that, almost no one on the force wanted anything to do with him. No one wanted to be his partner for daily assignments. Conversations stopped whenever he entered a room. One day a

fellow cop even pulled a switchblade on him while a dozen other officers stood by and watched.

13   During that period, Serpico almost gave up. He had risked his career and endangered his own life in an effort to improve the system. Yet it appeared that little was going to change. He had hoped that the department could clean itself up, but clearly that was not the case. So, in desperation, Serpico decided to make his allegations public. Early in 1970, he took his story to the *New York Times*.

14   When people read Serpico's story in the newspaper, they were outraged. The public demanded a full-scale investigation. As a result, a special commission was created to look into the widespread problem of crime within the police force. The commission conducted the most thorough probe in the history of the New York Police Department. As a result, stricter rules were developed to help prevent police corruption in the future. Many of the top officials who had refused to cooperate with Serpico were eventually forced to resign.

15   While all that was happening, Frank Serpico went on trying to be a good cop. He was transferred to the narcotics division in Brooklyn South, and he worked hard to combat the drug trade that flourished there. But again he met with resistance and distrust from his fellow officers. Again he encountered cops who were taking bribes from local criminals. Although in Brooklyn South he worked with three partners, he didn't

really trust any of them. In fact, on the night he was shot in the head, he felt that none of his partners rushed to help him.

16   It took Serpico months to recover from the bullet wound he suffered that night. Though he remained deaf in his left ear and unable to walk without a cane, his recovery was remarkable. As he regained his strength, however, he realized that his life was a shambles. He had sacrificed his future for the sake of his ideals. He had never stopped trying to be a good cop, but the effort had cost him dearly. After thinking it over, Frank Serpico decided not to return to the New York Police Department. Instead, he left the country to try to sort out his shattered life.

17   Serpico had discovered that fighting for right and justice can be difficult and lonely. He had suffered greatly for the sake of his values. But through his perseverance he had righted some wrongs. He had made a difference. 🍃

If you have been timed while reading this article, enter your reading time below. Then turn to the Words-per-Minute Table on page 195 and look up your reading speed (words per minute). Enter your reading speed on the graph on page 196.

Reading Time: **Lesson 16**

_____ : _____
Minutes   Seconds

A Finding the Main Idea

One statement below expresses the main idea of the article. One statement is too general, or too broad. The other statement explains only part of the article; it is too narrow. Label the statements using the following key:

M—Main Idea   **B—Too Broad**   **N—Too Narrow**

_____ 1. Frank Serpico was a man who had high ideals and paid dearly for trying to uphold them.

_____ 2. Frank Serpico forced New York City public officials to form a commission to investigate corruption in the police department.

_____ 3. Frank Serpico was an extremely honest cop who fought corruption in the New York Police Department and suffered for his efforts.

_____ Score 15 points for a correct M answer.

_____ Score 5 points for each correct B or N answer.

_____ **Total Score:** Finding the Main Idea

B Recalling Facts

How well do you remember the facts in the article? Put an X in the box next to the answer that correctly completes each statement about the article.

1. To Frank Serpico, being a cop meant
   ☐ a. having a good, steady job.
   ☐ b. protecting honest citizens against criminals.
   ☐ c. the chance to become a famous hero.

2. When Serpico first became aware of the corruption on the police force, he
   ☐ a. tried to ignore it.
   ☐ b. asked to be transferred to a new division.
   ☐ c. reported his findings to his division captain.

3. Serpico decided to go to higher authorities when
   ☐ a. a cop handed him an envelope containing $300.
   ☐ b. a fellow officer pulled a switchblade on him.
   ☐ c. he found police officers accepting free meals from restaurants in return for favors.

4. As a result of the *New York Times* article,
   ☐ a. eight plainclothes cops were arrested.
   ☐ b. a special commission was formed to look into the problem of corruption on the police force.
   ☐ c. Serpico decided to retire from the police force.

5. When Serpico was shot, he was a member of the
   ☐ a. 81st Precinct.
   ☐ b. Department of Investigation.
   ☐ c. Brooklyn South narcotics division.

Score 5 points for each correct answer.

_____ **Total Score:** Recalling Facts

C | Making Inferences

When you combine your own experience and information from a text to draw a conclusion that is not directly stated in that text, you are making an inference. Below are five statements that may or may not be inferences based on information in the article. Label the statements using the following key:

C—Correct Inference   F—Faulty Inference

_____ 1. Serpico ignored the small bribes he witnessed at first because he hoped it was not a serious problem.

_____ 2. Serpico thought it was all right for cops to take bribes as long as the bribes were only for traffic violations.

_____ 3. Police departments everywhere have serious problems with corruption.

_____ 4. Frank Serpico was the only good cop on the New York Police force.

_____ 5. If Serpico had not gone to the *New York Times,* a full-scale investigation would not have been conducted.

Score 5 points for each correct answer.

_____ **Total Score:** Making Inferences

D | Using Words Precisely

Each numbered sentence below contains an underlined word or phrase from the article. Following the sentence are three definitions. One definition is closest to the meaning of the underlined word. One definition is opposite or nearly opposite. Label those two definitions using the following key. Do not label the remaining definition.

C—Closest   O—Opposite or Nearly Opposite

1. Inside was a greeting card bearing the printed message, "<u>Recuperate</u> Quickly."

_____ a. get well

_____ b. cheer up

_____ c. become sicker

2. Serpico <u>pondered</u> the situation for months.

_____ a. forgot about

_____ b. ignored

_____ c. considered carefully

3. A small investigation was made into his <u>allegations</u> of graft and corruption.

_____ a. denials

_____ b. claims

_____ c. crimes

4. He was transferred to the narcotics division in Brooklyn South, and he worked hard to combat the drug trade that <u>flourished</u> there.

_____ a. was dying out

_____ b. thrived

_____ c. was conducted illegally

5. As he regained his strength, however, he realized that his life was a <u>shambles</u>.

_____ a. well-ordered

_____ b. mess

_____ c. unfulfilling

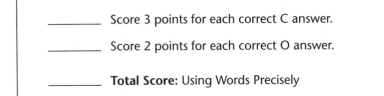

_____ Score 3 points for each correct C answer.

_____ Score 2 points for each correct O answer.

_____ **Total Score:** Using Words Precisely

Enter the four total scores in the spaces below, and add them together to find your Reading Comprehension Score. Then record your score on the graph on page 197.

Score	Question Type	Lesson 16
_____	Finding the Main Idea	
_____	Recalling Facts	
_____	Making Inferences	
_____	Using Words Precisely	
_____	**Reading Comprehension Score**	

Author's Approach

Put an X in the box next to the correct answer.

1. The main purpose of the first paragraph is to

☐ a. inform the reader about corruption in the New York Police Department.

☐ b. express an opinion about police work in New York.

☐ c. describe the injuries suffered in the line of duty by Frank Serpico.

2. From the statements below, choose the one that you believe the author would agree with.

☐ a. Frank Serpico was a squealer.

☐ b. Serpico felt it was his duty to report police department corruption.

☐ c. Many of the other officers in the police department secretly supported Serpico's war on corruption.

3. In this article, "He had sacrificed his future for the sake of his ideals" means

☐ a. Serpico had no future with the New York Police Department.

☐ b. Serpico believed whole-heartedly in his convictions.

☐ c. Serpico had made his life harder by upholding his beliefs.

4. Choose the statement below that best describes the author's position in paragraph 17.

☐ a. Serpico should be honored for his battle against corruption.

☐ b. Serpico didn't do enough to right wrongs in the department.

☐ c. Serpico was defeated in his fight for justice.

_____ Number of correct answers

Record your personal assessment of your work on the Critical Thinking Chart on page 198.

Summarizing and Paraphrasing

Put an X in the box next to the correct answer for question 2. Follow the directions provided for the other question.

1. Reread paragraph 8 in the article. Below, write a summary of the paragraph in no more than 25 words.

_____

_____

_____

_____

Reread your summary and decide if the summary covers important parts of the paragraph. Next, decide how to shorten the summary to 15 words or less without leaving out any essential information. Write this summary below.

_____

_____

_____

2. Choose the best one-sentence paraphrase for the following sentence from the article:

"Those few officers who weren't taking money simply looked the other way while their partners got richer and richer."

☐ a. The honest police officers tried not to watch when their partners accepted bribes.

☐ b. The police officers who didn't take bribes ignored the corruption going on around them.

☐ c. A couple of police officers stood guard while their partners received a bribe.

_____ Number of correct answers

Record your personal assessment of your work on the Critical Thinking Chart on page 198.

Critical Thinking

Put an X in the box next to the correct answer for questions 1, 2, and 5. Follow the directions provided for the other questions.

1. Which of the following statements from the article is an opinion rather than a fact?

☐ a. "Only a member of the New York Police Department would have sent such a vicious message."

☐ b. "Worst of all, most of the officers in the precinct accepted bribes."

☐ c. "Serpico knew that most of the men and women in the department hated him, or at least mistrusted him."

2. Based on Frank Serpico's actions as told in this article, you can predict that

☐ a. Serpico would rejoin the New York Police Department in the near future.

☐ b. the New York Police Department today would not be as corrupt as it was in the 1970s.

☐ c. Serpico would seek revenge against his fellow police officers.

3. Choose from the letters below to correctly complete the following statement. Write the letters on the lines.

On the positive side, _____, but on the negative side _____.

a. Serpico uncovered a major crime problem within the New York Police Department

b. Serpico was forced to flee the country

c. Serpico's life was shattered by his fight for justice

4. Think about cause–effect relationships in the article. Fill in the blanks in the cause–effect chart, drawing from the letters below.

Cause	Effect
Serpico refused to take bribes.	_____
Serpico told his story to the *New York Times*.	_____
_____	Serpico remained disabled.

a. Serpico was shot in the head while trying to arrest a heroin dealer.

b. The public demanded a full investigation.

c. Many police officers were suspicious of Serpico.

5. Of the following theme categories, which would this story fit into?

☐ a. Good usually triumphs over evil.

☐ b. One person can make a difference.

☐ c. Money is the root of all evil.

_____ Number of correct answers

Record your personal assessment of your work on the Critical Thinking Chart on page 198.

Personal Response

I can't believe

_____

_____

Self-Assessment

Before reading this article, I already knew

_____

_____

_____

_____

NELLIE BLY
Exposing the Truth

It was the most dangerous assignment Nellie Bly was ever offered. In 1888, Joseph Pulitzer, owner of the famous newspaper *The World,* asked her to write an article for his paper. He wanted her to investigate rumors of cruelty and neglect in the New York City insane asylum on Blackwells Island. The hospital was designed to care for insane people who had no money for private treatment. There had recently been stories of patient abuse at the hospital. But because doctors would not let reporters talk to the patients, no one knew if the stories were accurate. The only way for Nellie to learn the truth was to become a patient herself. That meant she had to pretend she was crazy.

2 Nellie was willing to do that because she knew it might help those who were mentally ill. But she was worried about one thing. If she succeeded in getting into the hospital, how would she ever get out? Joseph Pulitzer told her not to worry; he promised he would take care of that. But when Nellie asked him what he intended to do, he admitted that he didn't know.

Blackwells Island Workhouse about the time Nellie Bly exposed the miserable conditions in the asylum. This photograph was taken by Jacob Riis in 1890.

He told her she would just have to trust him. Although Nellie feared that she might end up trapped behind the walls of the insane asylum forever, she agreed to go ahead with the assignment. It was her only chance to uncover the truth.

3   After agreeing to write the article, she went to a boardinghouse and rented a room. As soon as she moved in, she began to roll her eyes and act strangely. She claimed she could not remember her own name, and she accused everyone in the boardinghouse of being crazy. Within a few hours she had frightened the landlady and all the other boarders. The landlady called the police, who took Nellie to a nearby hospital for an examination. Nellie was not sure she could fool trained professionals into thinking she was insane, but to her surprise, the doctors asked her only a few very basic questions. Then they concluded that she was, indeed, hopelessly insane.

4   Because it appeared that Nellie didn't have any money, the doctors put her on a boat and shipped her off to the insane asylum on Blackwells Island. When the boat landed and she stepped ashore, a guard grabbed her. Pretending to be confused, she asked where she was. "This is a place for insane people," the guard snarled, "and you'll never leave it."

Although Nellie believed that Joseph Pulitzer would do his best to get her released, those words still sent a shiver down her spine.

5   After being admitted to the hospital, Nellie immediately dropped her disguise and started acting perfectly normal. She wanted to see how the staff would react when they realized one of their patients was not sick. To her amazement, no one noticed. When she approached a doctor to talk to him, he ignored her. The same thing happened when she tried to start a conversation with a nurse. It didn't seem to matter what Nellie said or did— everyone just assumed that her actions were those of a crazy person.

6   Nellie soon learned that the staff did not pay much attention to any of the patients. She had expected medical care at the hospital to be minimal, but she was not prepared for the kind of heartless treatment that she saw all around her. Doctors routinely ignored the requests and complaints of the patients. Nurses beat those who were uncooperative. Sometimes staff members even banged patients' heads against a wall for no reason at all.

7   Nellie was equally stunned by the filthy living conditions that prevailed throughout the hospital. Once a week

nurses forced her and the other female patients to take baths in ice-cold water. In the evenings guards locked them up in tiny, unheated rooms. The staff made them sleep in thin little slips and would not give them any blankets. In the daytime nurses tied all the patients

Nellie Bly in 1890

together with ropes and led them outside like cattle for "outdoor exercise." Meals consisted of nothing more than bread, tea, and a few shriveled prunes. When Nellie tried to eat the bread, she found that it was old and stale. One morning she even found a spider in it.

8   After a couple of days in that inhumane environment, Nellie was ready to get out. When she tried to explain to a doctor that she was not sick, he simply laughed and walked away. There was nothing she could do but wait and hope that Joseph Pulitzer would keep his promise to get her released. Finally, after 10 days, Pulitzer came through. He sent a lawyer to Blackwells Island to arrange for Nellie's release. In order to get her out, the lawyer said that some of Nellie's friends had agreed to pay for private treatment.

9   As soon as Nellie was freed, she began to work on her story. When she finished, Pulitzer ran it on the front page of *The World*. The story instantly created a scandal, stirring the public's concern for the mentally ill. Health inspectors made a complete tour of the asylum and ordered the staff to improve conditions. Doctors at other hospitals began to conduct more careful examinations before declaring a person insane, and New York City increased its budget for care of the mentally ill by $1 million.

10   Nellie was delighted that her newspaper article helped to change the city's attitude toward the mentally ill. She was also happy that Joseph Pulitzer liked her work. He was so impressed, in fact, that he offered her a permanent job as a reporter for *The World*. That made her the first female reporter on Pulitzer's staff.

11   Nellie went on to write many other compelling newspaper articles. Among them were articles that exposed the poor treatment of factory workers and the struggles of the new labor unions. As one of the first women in her field, she also led the way for other female journalists. When she died in 1922, New York newspapers mourned the death of "the best reporter in America."

If you have been timed while reading this article, enter your reading time below. Then turn to the Words-per-Minute Table on page 195 and look up your reading speed (words per minute). Enter your reading speed on the graph on page 196.

Reading Time: Lesson 17

_____ : _____

Minutes   *Seconds*

A Finding the Main Idea

One statement below expresses the main idea of the article. One statement is too general, or too broad. The other statement explains only part of the article; it is too narrow. Label the statements using the following key:

M—Main Idea   **B—Too Broad**   **N—Too Narrow**

_____ 1. Nellie Bly posed as a mentally ill person to get into the insane asylum on Blackwells Island.

_____ 2. Nellie Bly uncovered and exposed the horrors on Blackwells Island, and went on to become a great newspaper reporter.

_____ 3. Nellie Bly was one of the greatest newspaper reporters of the late nineteenth and early twentieth centuries.

_____ Score 15 points for a correct M answer.

_____ Score 5 points for each correct B or N answer.

_____ **Total Score:** Finding the Main Idea

B Recalling Facts

How well do you remember the facts in the article? Put an X in the box next to the answer that correctly completes each statement about the article.

1. The insane asylum on Blackwells Island was intended for

☐ a. poor people who were physically ill.

☐ b. poor people who were mentally ill.

☐ c. old people who had no money.

2. When Nellie stopped acting crazy, the doctors and nurses

☐ a. became suspicious.

☐ b. didn't notice.

☐ c. put spiders in her food to frighten her.

3. When Nellie tried to talk to the doctors and nurses in the hospital, they

☐ a. beat her.

☐ b. ignored her.

☐ c. locked her in an unheated room.

4. Nellie stayed in the insane asylum

☐ a. 10 days.

☐ b. five days.

☐ c. two days.

5. As a result of Nellie's article, New York City

☐ a. closed the hospital on Blackwells Island.

☐ b. arrested the doctors at the asylum.

☐ c. began spending more money on the mentally ill.

Score 5 points for each correct answer.

_____ **Total Score:** Recalling Facts

C Making Inferences

When you combine your own experience and information from a text to draw a conclusion that is not directly stated in that text, you are making an inference. Below are five statements that may or may not be inferences based on information in the article. Label the statements using the following key:

C—Correct Inference   F—Faulty Inference

_____ 1. The doctors who declared Nellie insane did not know much about mental illness.

_____ 2. If Joseph Pulitzer's lawyer hadn't made arrangements to have Nellie released, she might never have gotten off Blackwells Island.

_____ 3. The doctors and nurses at the insane asylum didn't have any respect for people who were mentally ill.

_____ 4. Only a very good actress could have fooled the doctors into thinking she was crazy.

_____ 5. Nellie Bly was the first person seriously interested in finding out what conditions were like on Blackwells Island.

Score 5 points for each correct answer.

_____ **Total Score:** Making Inferences

D Using Words Precisely

Each numbered sentence below contains an underlined word or phrase from the article. Following the sentence are three definitions. One definition is closest to the meaning of the underlined word. One definition is opposite or nearly opposite. Label those two definitions using the following key. Do not label the remaining definition.

C—Closest   O—Opposite or Nearly Opposite

1. She had expected medical care at the hospital to be <u>minimal</u>, but she was not prepared for the kind of heartless treatment that she saw all around her.

_____ a. barely satisfactory

_____ b. inexpensive

_____ c. of the highest quality

2. Nellie was equally stunned by the filthy living conditions that <u>prevailed</u> throughout the hospital.

_____ a. were common

_____ b. were rare

_____ c. were concealed

3. After a couple of days in that <u>inhumane</u> environment, Nellie was ready to get out.

_____ a. unhealthy

_____ b. caring

_____ c. cruel

4. The story instantly created a <u>scandal</u>, stirring the public's concern for the mentally ill.

_____ a. public disgrace

_____ b. occasion for awarding an honor

_____ c. crisis

5. Nellie went on to write other <u>compelling</u> newspaper reports.

_____ a. lengthy

_____ b. ineffective

_____ c. demanding attention

_____ Score 3 points for each correct C answer.

_____ Score 2 points for each correct O answer.

_____ **Total Score:** Using Words Precisely

Enter the four total scores in the spaces below, and add them together to find your Reading Comprehension Score. Then record your score on the graph on page 197.

Score	Question Type	Lesson 17
_____	Finding the Main Idea	
_____	Recalling Facts	
_____	Making Inferences	
_____	Using Words Precisely	
_____	**Reading Comprehension Score**	

Author's Approach

Put an X in the box next to the correct answer.

1. The author uses the first sentence of the article to

☐ a. tell the reader about journalism in 1888.

☐ b. make the reader interested in learning about Nellie Bly.

☐ c. entertain the reader with Nellie Bly's adventures.

2. Based on the statement from the article, "Although Nellie feared that she might end up trapped behind the walls of the insane asylum forever, she agreed to go ahead with the assignment," you can conclude that the author wants the reader to think that

☐ a. Nellie was very trusting.

☐ b. Nellie was terrified by her dangerous assignment.

☐ c. Nellie was willing to risk her life to get a story.

3. How is the author's purpose for writing the article expressed in paragraph 9?

☐ a. The author expresses an opinion about the conditions in insane asylums in the late 1800s.

☐ b. The author informs the reader about the conditions in insane asylums in the late 1800s.

☐ c. The author describes the effect Nellie's story had on the public.

4. The author tells this story mainly by

☐ a. retelling one of Nellie's experiences as a journalist.

☐ b. comparing Nellie to modern journalists.

☐ c. telling different stories about Nellie Bly's experiences.

_____ Number of correct answers

Record your personal assessment of your work on the Critical Thinking Chart on page 198.

Summarizing and Paraphrasing

Put an X in the box next to the correct answer for questions 1 and 3. Follow the directions provided for the other question.

1. Below are summaries of the article. Choose the summary that says all the most important things about the article but in the fewest words.

☐ a. Journalist Nellie Bly became a patient in an insane asylum in order to expose the inhumane conditions there.

☐ b. Joseph Pulitzer asked Nellie Bly to investigate and write about an insane asylum for his newspaper. Nellie wrote the article, describing her own experiences in the asylum.

☐ c. Nellie Bly pretended to be insane so that she could become a patient in an asylum.

2. Reread paragraph 7 in the article. Below, write a summary of the paragraph in no more than 25 words.

_____

_____

_____

Reread your summary and decide whether it covers the important ideas in the paragraph. Next, decide how to shorten the summary to 15 words or less without leaving out any essential information. Write this summary below.

_____

_____

3. Read the following statement about the article. Then read the paraphrase of that statement. Choose the reason that best tells why the paraphrase does not say the same thing as the statement.

Statement: Even when Nellie behaved and spoke like a reasonable person, the doctors and nurses at Blackwells Island refused to listen to her.

Paraphrase: The doctors and nurses at Blackwells Island were too busy to listen to Nellie.

☐ a. Paraphrase says too much.

☐ b. Paraphrase doesn't say enough.

☐ c. Paraphrase doesn't agree with the statement about the article.

_____ Number of correct answers

Record your personal assessment of your work on the Critical Thinking Chart on page 198.

Critical Thinking

Put an X in the box next to the correct answer for questions 2 and 4. Follow the directions provided for the other questions.

1. For each statement below, write O if it expresses an opinion and write F if it expresses a fact.

_____ a. The doctors and nurses at Blackwells Island were often cruel to their patients.

_____ b. At the time of her death in 1922, Nelly Bly was the best reporter in America.

_____ c. Patients admitted to Blackwells Island before 1888 had difficulty obtaining a release.

2. Based on the information in paragraph 11, you can predict that

☐ a. Nellie would pose as a factory worker to learn about labor unions.

☐ b. Nellie's success would make it easier for other women to work in journalism.

☐ c. male journalists would resent Nellie's success.

3. Choose from the letters below to correctly complete the following statement. Write the letters on the lines.

According to the article, Nellie's story about Blackwells Island caused _____ to _____, and the effect was _____.

a. show concern for the mentally ill

b. the public

c. health inspectors toured the asylum

4. If you were a journalist, how could you use the information in the article to investigate a story?

☐ a. Like Nellie, make sure you have the newspaper owner's support.

☐ b. Like Nellie, get as close to your subject as you can.

☐ c. Like Nellie, pretend to be insane.

5. In which paragraph did you find your information or details to answer question 3?

_____

_____ Number of correct answers

Record your personal assessment of your work on the Critical Thinking Chart on page 198.

Personal Response

Begin the first 5–8 sentences of your own article about someone's efforts to uncover the truth. It may tell of a real experience or one that is imagined.

_____

_____

_____

_____

Self-Assessment

I can't really understand how

_____

_____

_____

_____

CRITICAL THINKING

ANIMALS TO THE RESCUE
Caring Creatures

Thank goodness someone had a camera. Otherwise, no one would have believed it. On August 16, 1996, a three-year-old boy was visiting the Brookfield Zoo in Illinois with his parents when he somehow crawled over a three-foot wall. He lost his balance and fell 18 feet into a gorilla habitat.

2   "The gorilla's got my baby!" the boy's mother shouted. Bystanders stared helplessly down into the Tropic World exhibit where the little boy lay on the concrete floor, unconscious. The child was totally at the mercy of the gorillas. "I feared the worst," said Jeff Bruno, a paramedic who rushed to the scene.

3   But then something amazing happened. One of the gorillas went over to the boy, picked him up, and cradled him in her arms. The gorilla was Binti Jua, an eight-year-old female who weighed 160 pounds. She held the boy tenderly, protecting him from the other gorillas in the compound. "I could not believe how gentle she was," said Celeste Lombardi, a zoo worker who had helped to raise Binti Jua.

4   With Koola, her own 18-month-old daughter on her back, Binti Jua carefully

Animals such as dogs, gorillas, dolphins and even parrots have performed heroic acts in order to save humans from dangerous situations.

carried the boy to a service door where zoo workers were waiting. The boy, whose parents requested that his name not be released, was badly injured. He had a broken hand, some cuts, and minor bruising to the brain. But after several days in the hospital, he was back home. Meanwhile, Binti Jua, whose name is Swahili for "daughter of sunshine," became a national hero. Gifts of money—and bananas—poured into the zoo in honor of the gentle gorilla.

5 No one knows for certain why Binti Jua rescued the boy. Perhaps she was simply following some animal instinct. Or perhaps her actions stemmed from her past contact with humans. As an infant, Binti Jua had been rejected by her own mother; from age two months, she had been raised by humans. These same trainers had taught Binti Jua how to be a good mother, including how to bring Koola to the service door so zoo workers could monitor the baby's health. Jack Hanna, director of the Columbus Zoo, commented that when Binti Jua saw the child lying in the habitat, "she knew from humans taking care of her that they could take care of this problem." In any case, Binti Jua's extraordinary act saved the little boy's life.

6 Binti Jua is not the only animal to surprise people with its heroism. In India recently, a wild monkey saved a human baby from drowning. A woman was crossing a makeshift bridge when she slipped, dropping her baby into the rapids below. The mother screamed in panic, but there was nothing she could do. It seemed certain her child would perish. Suddenly, from among the trees at the edge of the water, a monkey dove into the river. The monkey grabbed the baby, pulled it ashore, and returned it to the arms of the shocked but grateful mother.

7 In a small Italian town, a parrot performed a different but equally stunning life-saving maneuver. The parrot belonged to a family that included a one-year-old child. One day the child toddled out into the street just as a truck came barreling along. The baby's mother cried out, but she was too far away to save her child. The parrot, however, flew off its perch and went straight toward the truck. By flying right in front of the windshield, the bird blocked the driver's view and forced him to slam on the brakes. The truck came to a stop just a few feet from the baby.

8 Dolphins, too, have rescued people in trouble. In Australia, some teenagers were surfing in the Pacific Ocean near a school of dolphins. As one of the boys cruised along on his surfboard, he suddenly spotted a tiger shark coming directly for him. The shark struck quickly, biting a huge hole in the surfboard, knocking the boy into the water, and wounding him. But as the shark circled around for the kill, the dolphins intervened. They charged at the shark and drove it off, leaving the boy frightened and injured, but glad to be alive.

Binti Jua, the gorilla who saved a three-year-old boy, and her 17-month-old baby Koola

9   The most common animal hero of all is the dog. There are many cases of dogs risking their lives to save humans. In fact, such dogs even have their own award—the Ken-L Ration Dog Hero of the Year award.

10   One winner was an American pit bull named Weela. She lived with Lori and Daniel Walkins and their son, Gary, in California. The Walkins had a home in the Tijuana River Valley. In the winter of 1993, that region was hit with several drenching rains. The river, usually little more than a trickle, became a torrent about a mile across.

11   One day the Walkins family noticed about 30 people, including small children and babies, getting ready to cross the river. "We knew the water was deep and the currents treacherous," said Lori. "We tried to yell," she added, "but they apparently didn't understand English." The Walkins, who were too far away to stop them, thought for sure the people would wade into the river and drown.

12   Then Weela raced forward toward the riverbank, barking and growling. The snapping pit bull got everybody's attention. She guarded the river so ferociously that no one could cross. Weela kept up her act until the Walkins scrambled down to the river. They then took the people downstream to a safer crossing point.

13   Another dog saved the life of 10-year-old Josh Coffey. On March 6, 1996, Josh didn't come to supper when his mother called. The boy, who had been playing with a couple of stray dogs when it started to snow, had somehow become disoriented and wandered away from his home. Hundreds of neighbors gathered to search for the lost boy. For three days, they scoured the hills of Cassville, Missouri. During that time, the wind chill dropped to 34 degrees below zero.

14   Finally, on March 9, a searcher came across one of the stray dogs. The barking dog led the man to a spot where Josh was lying face down in the snow. The other dog was standing guard over the boy. Miraculously, Josh—who had no gloves or hat—was still alive. The dogs had used their warm bodies to keep him from freezing to death.

15   And then there was King, a five-year-old dog belonging to Howard and Fran Carlson and their little daughter, Pearl. On December 22, 1980, the Carlsons were sleeping peacefully in their beds when the house erupted in flames. King rushed into Pearl's room and tugged on her pajama sleeve until she finally woke up. Pearl then stumbled through the heavy smoke to rouse her parents. Howard, who suffered from lung disease, had recently been discharged from the hospital; he didn't have much strength. Frantically, Fran helped him over to a window and told him to jump. Then she hurried after Pearl, who had run into the living room. Fran grabbed Pearl and the two escaped through a living room window.

16   Fran was about to collapse with relief when she spotted King, still in the house, standing in front of an open window. Although he was trying to bark, all he could manage was a thin squeak. Fran ordered him to jump, but he refused. That was when she realized her husband was nowhere in sight. She raced back inside and discovered Howard lying semiconscious on the floor. Fortunately, she was able to get him out of the building in time.

17   It wasn't until the next morning that the Carlsons fully understood what King had done. As he ran through the burning house, flames had singed his hair and burned his paws. His metal collar had gotten so hot that it burned his throat. And at one point in the rescue, he had actually gnawed through a plywood door. That explained why he couldn't bark; he had wood splinters lodged in his throat.

18   Why are people surprised by the heroic actions of animals? Perhaps it is because they do not expect animals to understand human needs. Perhaps they do not think animals are capable of helping humans unless they are trained to do so. Whatever the reason, people are often amazed by animal heroics; they are also often touched and grateful. 🍃

If you have been timed while reading this article, enter your reading time below. Then turn to the Words-per-Minute Table on page 195 and look up your reading speed (words per minute). Enter your reading speed on the graph on page 196.

Reading Time: Lesson 18

_____ : _____

Minutes   Seconds

A Finding the Main Idea

One statement below expresses the main idea of the article. One statement is too general, or too broad. The other statement explains only part of the article; it is too narrow. Label the statements using the following key:

M—Main Idea   **B—Too Broad**   **N—Too Narrow**

_____ 1. Often risking their own lives, many different kinds of animals have performed incredible acts of heroism to rescue people's lives.

_____ 2. Many animals have performed heroic acts.

_____ 3. An eight-year-old gorilla saved the life of a small boy who had fallen into the gorilla habitat at the Brookfield Zoo.

_____ Score 15 points for a correct M answer.

_____ Score 5 points for each correct B or N answer.

_____ **Total Score:** Finding the Main Idea

B Recalling Facts

How well do you remember the facts in the article? Put an X in the box next to the answer that correctly completes each statement about the article.

1. Binti Jua carried the little boy who had fallen into the gorilla exhibit to
    - ☐ a. a service door where zoo workers were waiting.
    - ☐ b. the child's frightened mother.
    - ☐ c. the hospital.

2. A parrot in Italy rescued a baby by
    - ☐ a. saving the child from drowning in a river.
    - ☐ b. pulling the child from a burning building.
    - ☐ c. flying in front of a truck that was about to hit the child.

3. A teenage surfer in Australia was rescued from a shark attack by
    - ☐ a. dolphins.
    - ☐ b. a dog.
    - ☐ c. a wild monkey.

4. Two stray dogs used their bodies to
    - ☐ a. save 30 people from a deep, treacherous river.
    - ☐ b. keep Josh Coffey from freezing to death.
    - ☐ c. rescue the Carlson family.

5. During the fire, King couldn't bark because
    - ☐ a. flames had singed his hair and burned his paws.
    - ☐ b. his metal collar had burned his throat.
    - ☐ c. he had splinters lodged in his throat.

Score 5 points for each correct answer.

_____ **Total Score:** Recalling Facts

C | Making Inferences

When you combine your own experience and information from a text to draw a conclusion that is not directly stated in that text, you are making an inference. Below are five statements that may or may not be inferences based on information in the article. Label the statements using the following key:

C—Correct Inference   **F—Faulty Inference**

_____ 1. All dogs are willing to risk their lives for their owners.

_____ 2. Pets that rescue their owners have received special training in life-saving techniques.

_____ 3. Binti Jua treated the little boy the way she had been taught to take care of her own baby.

_____ 4. King refused to leave the burning house because Howard Carlson was still inside it.

_____ 5. Weela barked and growled at the people by the river because they were on the Walkins' property.

Score 5 points for each correct answer.

_____ **Total Score:** Making Inferences

D | Using Words Precisely

Each numbered sentence below contains an underlined word or phrase from the article. Following the sentence are three definitions. One definition is closest to the meaning of the underlined word. One definition is opposite or nearly opposite. Label those two definitions using the following key. Do not label the remaining definition.

C—Closest   **O—Opposite or Nearly Opposite**

1. He lost his balance and fell 18 feet into a gorilla <u>habitat</u>.

_____ a. artificial environment

_____ b. natural surroundings

_____ c. cage

2. But as the shark circled around for the kill, the dolphins <u>intervened</u>.

_____ a. dove underwater

_____ b. moved away

_____ c. came between

3. The river, usually little more than a trickle, became a <u>torrent</u> about a mile across.

_____ a. shallow stream

_____ b. high wave

_____ c. rushing water

4. The boy, who had been playing with a couple of stray dogs when it started to snow, had somehow become <u>disoriented</u> and wandered away from his home.

_____ a. confused

_____ b. alert

_____ c. badly frightened

5. She raced back inside and discovered Howard lying <u>semiconscious</u> on the floor.

_____ a. attentive

_____ b. barely awake

_____ c. half burned

_____ Score 3 points for each correct C answer.

_____ Score 2 points for each correct O answer.

_____ **Total Score:** Using Words Precisely

Enter the four total scores in the spaces below, and add them together to find your Reading Comprehension Score. Then record your score on the graph on page 197.

Score	Question Type	Lesson 18
_____	Finding the Main Idea	
_____	Recalling Facts	
_____	Making Inferences	
_____	Using Words Precisely	
_____	**Reading Comprehension Score**	

Author's Approach

Put an X in the box next to the correct answer.

1. What is the author's purpose in writing "Animals to the Rescue: Caring Creatures"?

☐ a. To encourage the reader to be kind to animals

☐ b. To inform the reader about animals that have saved people's lives

☐ c. To emphasize the similarities between animals and humans

2. What does the author imply by saying "Weela kept up her act until the Walkins scrambled down to the river"?

☐ a. Weela was only pretending to be ferocious.

☐ b. The Walkins hurried because they feared that their dog might attack.

☐ c. Weela performed tricks until her owners arrived.

3. The author tells this story mainly by

☐ a. retelling personal experiences.

☐ b. comparing different topics.

☐ c. telling different stories about the same topic.

_____ Number of correct answers

Record your personal assessment of your work on the Critical Thinking Chart on page 198.

CRITICAL THINKING

Summarizing and Paraphrasing

Put an X in the box next to the correct answer for questions 1 and 3. Follow the directions provided for the other question.

1. Below are summaries of the article. Choose the summary that says all the most important things about the article but in the fewest words.

☐ a. Animals like Binti Jua, Weela, and King have performed heroic deeds to save human lives.

☐ b. Many animals have risked their own lives to save human lives.

☐ c. Gorillas, parrots, monkeys, dolphins, and dogs have all acted bravely to save human lives.

2. Reread paragraph 8 in the article. Below, write a summary of the paragraph in no more than 25 words.

_____

_____

_____

_____

Reread your summary and decide if the summary covers important parts of the paragraph. Next, decide how to shorten the summary to 15 words or less without leaving out any essential information. Write this summary below.

_____

_____

_____

3. Choose the sentence that correctly restates the following sentence from the article:

"Bystanders stared helplessly down into the Tropic World exhibit where the little boy lay on the concrete floor, unconscious."

☐ a. Witnesses could do nothing but watch as the child lay, senseless, on the exhibit floor.

☐ b. Witnesses did not try to help the boy after he fell onto the exhibit floor.

☐ c. Observers watched to see what would happen after the boy fell asleep on the exhibit floor.

_____ Number of correct answers

Record your personal assessment of your work on the Critical Thinking Chart on page 198.

Critical Thinking

Put an X in the box next to the correct answer for questions 1 and 4. Follow the directions provided for the other questions.

1. From the article, you can predict that if another child fell into the gorilla habitat,

☐ a. Binti Jua would ignore the child.

☐ b. Binti Jua would try to harm the child.

☐ c. Binti Jua would try to save the child.

2. Choose from the letters below to correctly complete the following statement. Write the letters on the lines.

In the article, _____ and _____ are alike.

a. the rescue of the Carlsons

b. the rescue of Josh Coffey

c. the rescue of the little boy in the Tropic World exhibit

3. Think about cause–effect relationships in the article. Fill in the blanks in the cause–effect chart, drawing from the letters below.

Cause	Effect
a child walked in front of a truck	_____
_____	a monkey saved the baby from drowning
_____	the Tijuana River became a torrent

   a. the region had had several drenching rains

   b. the family's parrot flew in front of the windshield

   c. a woman dropped her baby into a river

4. Of the following theme categories, which would this story fit into?

   ☐ a. A dog is a human's best friend.

   ☐ b. Animals are more intelligent than humans.

   ☐ c. Animals are loyal, caring creatures.

5. Which paragraphs from the article provide evidence that supports your answer to question 3?

   _____

   _____ Number of correct answers

   Record your personal assessment of your work on the Critical Thinking Chart on page 198.

Personal Response

Describe a time when an animal you know performed an act of heroism.

_____

_____

_____

_____

Self-Assessment

One of the things I did best when reading this article was

_____

_____

_____

I believe I did this well because

_____

_____

_____

_____

FLORENCE NIGHTINGALE
A Mission for Life

This illustration shows Florence Nightingale supervising the hospital at Scutari, Turkey, during the Crimean War, 1854.

The screams of wounded soldiers echoed through the corridors. Clogged sewer pipes filled the air with a foul stench. And in every room rats could be seen scurrying from corner to corner, rummaging among the dead bodies that lay scattered on the floor. That was the scene that greeted Florence Nightingale when she arrived at the English army hospital in Scutari, Turkey, on November 9, 1854.

2   Florence had come to take charge of the nursing of soldiers injured in the Crimean War. As England, France, and Turkey fought Russia for control of the Black Sea, wounded British soldiers were being sent to Scutari for treatment. But the Scutari Hospital was nothing but a huge old Turkish military barracks that was filthy and underfurnished. Supplies were inadequate, and conditions overall were deplorable. Before Florence arrived, there was no hot water, no soap, and no kitchen. There were no clean bandages, no candles or lamps and, worst of all, no nurses.

3   None of that surprised Florence. She had been warned that the hospital was a

shambles. But she had come to help anyway. She planned to fix up the place and improve care for the wounded. It was a task no one else wanted. In 1854, most people considered nursing to be a dirty business. Only poor, uneducated women became nurses. Most were criminals or alcoholics who agreed to work in a hospital to avoid going to jail. They were totally unfit to care for the sick.

4   Florence, on the other hand, came from a wealthy London family. She was educated mainly by her father who taught her Greek, Latin, French, German, Italian, history, philosophy, and mathematics. As a young girl she spent much of her time attending parties, concerts, and society balls. At the age of 17, though, she grew tired of her carefree lifestyle. She longed to devote her energies to something more important. Since she had always been interested in medicine and felt a special sympathy for sick people, she announced her intention of becoming a nurse.

5   That announcement shocked Florence's mother. Knowing the awful reputation of nurses, Mrs. Nightingale forbade her daughter to set foot in a hospital. For the next 16 years, Florence honored her mother's wishes, but she did not put aside her interest in the care of the sick. She educated herself by reading books and reports on medicine and public health.

Then in 1850 she took a full nurses' training course at a school in Germany. By 1853, she knew more about caring for the sick than any nurse in the country.

6   Although her mother still objected, Florence decided that the time had come to put her knowledge to use. In August she became head of a women's hospital in London. There she surprised the doctors by listening to the complaints and criticisms of the patients. She instituted reforms throughout the hospital and tried to provide the nurses with some basic training.

7   Florence was working there when the Crimean War broke out. When Sidney Herbert, the British Secretary of War, heard of the appalling conditions at Scutari Hospital, he knew something had to be done. Someone had to clean up the facilities there and organize proper care for the wounded. Herbert could think of only one person for the job: Florence Nightingale.

8   Herbert wrote to Florence, urging her to go to Scutari. Her friends tried to discourage her, but Florence readily agreed to go. She could not ignore the needs of the brave men who were fighting for their country. Rounding up 38 trained nurses to accompany her, she set off for Turkey.

9   When she arrived at the hospital, Florence expected a warm welcome from the doctors. Instead they were cool—even hostile. They were angry that the Secretary of War had sent a woman to interfere with their routine. They thought that Florence was nothing more than some fragile, high-bred woman who would be of no help to them at all.

10   It didn't take Florence long to prove the doctors wrong. On the day she

Florence Nightingale, known as the "Lady with the Lamp"

arrived, 500 wounded cavalry soldiers were brought in from a battle that had just been fought. The doctors worked frantically to treat the most severely wounded. Many men had been shot in the arm or the leg and needed to have the injured limb amputated before infection set in. Having no way to dispose of the severed limbs, the doctors simply threw them out the window. As the rotting arms and legs piled up in the hospital courtyard, the other nurses just stared in horror. But Florence quickly went to work. She found a hospital attendant with an old army cart and arranged to have the pile hauled away and buried.

11   Over the next few days Florence set up three kitchens and a laundry. She also organized a cleaning crew to scrub the entire building. Using her own money, she bought bandages, sheets, operating tables, pots and pans, lamps, towels, and silverware. This was the first time in history that wounded soldiers received good hospital care.

12   Florence herself assisted doctors even during the bloodiest operations. And she never avoided patients with contagious diseases. She knew she was risking her own health by having contact with those soldiers. Still, she spent hours by their bedsides, nursing them back to health. "She was so brave herself," one soldier said, "she gave us all courage."

13   Before long Florence had won the admiration of every patient in the hospital. Despite her hectic schedule, she always found time to visit the wards where the soldiers slept. Usually she went at night when she had finished the rest of her work. To light her way along the four miles of corridors, she carried a small lamp. The soldiers loved to see her coming. Many were young boys, only 15 or 16 years old, and often they were in too much pain to sleep. As they lay in the dark and lonely ward, they watched for the woman they called "The Lady with the Lamp." "What comfort we felt to see her," one soldier said. "We kissed her shadow as she passed."

14   Florence was so successful in organizing the Scutari Hospital that she was put in charge of all the British army hospitals in the Crimea. When the Crimean War ended in 1856, Florence returned to England a national hero. But she did not want public acclaim. She established a quiet, private life devoted to further work in the field of health care.

15   But her years in Turkey had taken their toll. The hard work and constant exposure to disease had permanently weakened her health. Within a few years of her return to England, she was an invalid. But that did not stop her from working. She wrote several books and founded a school for nurses. She took care of her correspondence, research, and writing from a couch in her London home. She also received many visitors. She was considered an authority on the care of the sick, and her advice was sought by important people the world over. The United States even asked her advice for setting up field hospitals during the Civil War.

16   Florence Nightingale accomplished a great deal in her life. She single-handedly transformed nursing from a lowly, unskilled job into a respectable, even noble, profession. She established an efficient and compassionate system for caring for the sick. And she won the undying gratitude of hundreds of thousands of young English soldiers. In 1907, Florence Nightingale was awarded the British Order of Merit. She was the first woman ever to receive that honor.

If you have been timed while reading this article, enter your reading time below. Then turn to the Words-per-Minute Table on page 195 and look up your reading speed (words per minute). Enter your reading speed on the graph on page 196.

Reading Time: Lesson 19

_____ : _____
Minutes   Seconds

A | Finding the Main Idea

One statement below expresses the main idea of the article. One statement is too general, or too broad. The other statement explains only part of the article; it is too narrow. Label the statements using the following key:

M—Main Idea　　　**B—Too Broad**　　　**N—Too Narrow**

_____ 1. Against the wishes of her upper-class family, Florence Nightingale studied health care and turned nursing into a scientific profession.

_____ 2. Florence Nightingale worked in a hospital for British soldiers in Turkey during the Crimean War and forever changed the way people looked at nurses.

_____ 3. Florence Nightingale's courage, organizational ability, and hard work greatly improved the way wounded soldiers were cared for and made nursing an honorable profession.

_____ Score 15 points for a correct M answer.

_____ Score 5 points for each correct B or N answer.

_____ **Total Score:** Finding the Main Idea

B | Recalling Facts

How well do you remember the facts in the article? Put an X in the box next to the answer that correctly completes each statement about the article.

1. In the early 1800s, most English nurses were
   □ a. well trained.
   □ b. criminals or alcoholics.
   □ c. in Turkey caring for soldiers wounded in the Crimean War.

2. When Florence first announced her intention to become a nurse, her mother
   □ a. enrolled her in a school for nurses.
   □ b. sent her to Scutari to study medicine.
   □ c. forbade her to set foot in a hospital.

3. Before going to Turkey, Florence
   □ a. spent time in a London hospital.
   □ b. knew nothing about medicine or public health.
   □ c. was head of a women's hospital.

4. When Florence arrived at Scutari Hospital, the doctors
   □ a. were unfriendly.
   □ b. gave her a warm welcome.
   □ c. were not doing anything for the wounded.

5. The Scutari Hospital was
   □ a. a training place for nurses.
   □ b. a Turkish barracks.
   □ c. an old factory.

Score 5 points for each correct answer.

_____ **Total Score:** Recalling Facts

C Making Inferences

When you combine your own experience and information from a text to draw a conclusion that is not directly stated in that text, you are making an inference. Below are five statements that may or may not be inferences based on information in the article. Label the statements using the following key:

C—Correct Inference   F—Faulty Inference

_____ 1. Florence Nightingale was an extremely good manager.

_____ 2. Before Florence Nightingale began changing the way nurses were trained, nursing was not considered an important profession.

_____ 3. The doctors at Scutari Hospital did not care whether the soldiers in their care lived or died.

_____ 4. Because of her decision to go into nursing, Florence Nightingale was rejected by upper-class British society.

_____ 5. If it hadn't been for the Crimean War, Florence would not have become concerned about the health care of soldiers.

Score 5 points for each correct answer.

_____ **Total Score:** Making Inferences

D Using Words Precisely

Each numbered sentence below contains an underlined word or phrase from the article. Following the sentence are three definitions. One definition is closest to the meaning of the underlined word. One definition is opposite or nearly opposite. Label those two definitions using the following key. Do not label the remaining definition.

C—Closest   O—Opposite or Nearly Opposite

1. For the next 16 years, Florence <u>honored</u> her mother's wishes, but she did not put aside her interest in the care of the sick.

_____ a. remembered

_____ b. respected

_____ c. rebelled against

2. She <u>instituted</u> reforms throughout the hospital and tried to provide the nurses with some basic training.

_____ a. questioned

_____ b. did away with

_____ c. established

3. Having no way to dispose of the <u>severed</u> limbs, the doctors simply threw them out the window.

_____ a. undivided or whole

_____ b. multiple

_____ c. cut off

4. When Sidney Herbert, the British Secretary of War, heard of the <u>appalling</u> conditions at Scutari Hospital, he knew something had to be done.

_____ a. dreadful

_____ b. daily

_____ c. appealing

5. Florence returned to England a national hero. But she did not want public <u>acclaim</u>.

_____ a. praise

_____ b. disapproval

_____ c. publicity

_____ Score 3 points for each correct C answer.

_____ Score 2 points for each correct O answer.

_____ **Total Score:** Using Words Precisely

Enter the four total scores in the spaces below, and add them together to find your Reading Comprehension Score. Then record your score on the graph on page 197.

Score	Question Type	Lesson 19
_____	Finding the Main Idea	
_____	Recalling Facts	
_____	Making Inferences	
_____	Using Words Precisely	
_____	**Reading Comprehension Score**	

Author's Approach

Put an X in the box next to the correct answer.

1. What does the author mean by the statement "But her years in Turkey had taken their toll"?

☐ a. Florence was nearly penniless because she had spent so much money on supplies for the hospital in Scutari.

☐ b. Florence was exhausted after working so hard in the hospital in Scutari.

☐ c. Florence had aged considerably after spending so many years in Turkey.

2. What is the author's purpose in writing "Florence Nightingale: A Mission for Life"?

☐ a. To inform the reader about Florence Nightingale's efforts to reform nursing

☐ b. To describe the filthy conditions in hospitals before Florence Nightingale reformed nursing

☐ c. To encourage the reader to consider nursing as a profession

3. Based on the statement from the article "There she surprised the doctors by listening to the complaints and criticisms of the patients," you can conclude that the author wants the reader to think that

☐ a. Florence could take better care of the patients than most doctors.

☐ b. most nurses at that time showed little concern for their patients.

☐ c. the patients frequently protested against the filthy conditions in the hospital.

4. The author tells this story mainly by

☐ a. comparing Florence's experiences at different hospitals.

☐ b. using his or her imagination and creativity.

☐ c. retelling Florence's experiences at one hospital.

_____ Number of correct answers

Record your personal assessment of your work on the Critical Thinking Chart on page 198.

Summarizing and Paraphrasing

Put an X in the box next to the correct answer.

1. Below are summaries of the article. Choose the summary that says all the most important things about the article but in the fewest words.

☐ a. During the Crimean War, Florence Nightingale instituted reforms in a hospital in Turkey.

☐ b. Florence Nightingale became a nurse at a time when the profession was not respected. Her work reforming the conditions in a Turkish hospital during the Crimean War helped transform nursing and the treatment of wounded soldiers.

☐ c. Florence Nightingale's reforms and her compassionate care of the wounded at a Turkish hospital during the Crimean War raised nursing from a lowly job to a respectable profession.

2. Read the following statement about the article. Then read the paraphrase of that statement. Choose the reason that best tells why the paraphrase does not say the same thing as the statement.

Statement: When Florence walked down the hospital corridors carrying her small lamp, the grateful soldiers kissed her shadow as she passed by.

Paraphrase: The wounded soldiers in the hospital in Scutari were so grateful for Florence's care and attention that, when she walked

down the corridor, they kissed the shadow cast by the small lamp she carried.

☐ a. Paraphrase says too much.

☐ b. Paraphrase doesn't say enough.

☐ c. Paraphrase doesn't agree with the statement about the article.

3. Choose the sentence that correctly restates the following sentence from the article:

"Knowing the awful reputation of nurses, Mrs. Nightingale forbade her daughter to set foot in a hospital."

☐ a. Mrs. Nightingale would not let her daughter become a nurse because the profession was not respected.

☐ b. Mrs. Nightingale would not let her daughter be treated in a hospital because nurses had such a bad reputation.

☐ c. When Florence hurt her foot, Mrs. Nightingale would not allow her daughter to walk into a hospital.

_____ Number of correct answers

Record your personal assessment of your work on the Critical Thinking Chart on page 198.

Critical Thinking

Put an X in the box next to the correct answer for questions 1 and 4. Follow the directions provided for the other questions.

1. Based on the events in the article, you can predict that the following will happen next:

☐ a. Florence Nightingale will be asked to travel to field hospitals on U.S. battlefields during the Civil War.

☐ b. In future wars, care for wounded soldiers will continue to improve because of Florence Nightingale's reforms.

☐ c. Florence Nightingale will go back to school to become a doctor.

CRITICAL THINKING

2. Choose from the letters below to correctly complete the following statement. Write the letters on the lines.

In the article, _____ and _____ are different.

a. the nursing methods Florence used at the women's hospital in London

b. the nursing methods Florence used at the hospital in Scutari

c. the nursing methods most British nurses used

3. Read paragraph 10. Then choose from the letters below to correctly complete the following statement. Write the letters on the lines.

According to paragraph 10, _____ because _____.

a. doctors had no way to dispose of the severed limbs

b. doctors knew that infection would set in

c. doctors threw amputated arms and legs out the window

4. If you were a nurse, how could you use the information in the article to take care of wounded soldiers in a field hospital?

☐ a. Make sure that conditions are sanitary.

☐ b. Carry a lamp when visiting patients.

☐ c. Use your own money to buy hospital supplies.

_____ Number of correct answers

Record your personal assessment of your work on the Critical Thinking Chart on page 198.

Personal Response

What was most surprising or interesting to you about this article?

_____

_____

_____

_____

Self-Assessment

From reading this article, I have learned

_____

_____

_____

_____

CRITICAL THINKING

MOTHER TERESA
Serving the Poorest of the Poor

When the people of India called her the "saint of the gutter," they meant it as high praise. The gutter was where Mother Teresa worked. Like all Catholic nuns, she had taken three sacred vows: to remain poor, to remain unmarried, and to obey the rules of the church. But Mother Teresa went beyond that. She took a fourth vow promising to provide "free service to the poorest of the poor." She found such people in the slums of Calcutta, India.

2   Even as a young girl growing up in Albania—where she was known as Agnes Bojaxhiu—this extraordinary individual knew her calling in life. She wanted to become a missionary. "At the age of 12, I first knew I had a vocation to help the poor," she later said. In 1928, at the age of 18, she answered the call. Agnes Bojaxhiu joined the Sisters of Loretto, a missionary order of Irish nuns. She took her new name from St. Thérèse, a 19th-century French nun.

3   After training in Ireland and India, Sister Teresa became a teacher in Calcutta. Eventually, she became the principal at St. Mary's High School. For many years, her

Mother Teresa dedicated her life to helping the poor. Here she comforts an infant in her orphanage in Calcutta, India.

life was safe and comfortable. She taught upper-class children and worked in nice, clean surroundings.

4   Then, on September 10, 1946, her life changed. By that time, Sister Teresa had lived in India for nearly 20 years, so, of course, she had witnessed the suffering of the poor. The poor were difficult to miss in Calcutta. Many were lying in the gutters just beyond the walls of her school. Every day Sister Teresa saw poor people dying of hunger and disease.

5   On this special day, however, she saw them in a different light. Sister Teresa was riding on a train when it suddenly hit her: she needed to do more. The knowledge came to her as a divine revelation, which she later described as "a call within a call." To her, the message was clear. "I was to give up all," she later wrote, "and follow Jesus into the slums."

6   It took two years for her to get the church's permission to leave St. Mary's. Generally, nuns were not allowed to leave their order and go out ministering on their own. If they wanted to do so, they were expected to give up their vocation and become laywomen. Sister Teresa, however, did not want to lose her identity as a nun. Luckily, the church finally allowed her to leave the Sisters of Loretto but still remain a nun.

7   On December 21, 1948, Sister Teresa walked into the slums to begin her new work. She spotted a cluster of half-naked children curled up in an alley. Right there, in that festering slum, Sister Teresa opened a new school. She taught the alphabet, using a stick to carve letters in the dust. The students were the ones who began calling her Mother Teresa.

8   Although Mother Teresa was gratified by the children's response, she felt she was not doing enough to help other poor people. Every day she saw Indians dying in the streets, many of them suffering from leprosy or some other terrible disease. One day Mother Teresa came across a dying woman whom she later described as "half-eaten by maggots and rats." She sat down next to her, gently stroking the woman's head until she died.

9   In giving comfort to the dying woman, Mother Teresa found her life's work. In 1950, she formed a new religious order, which she called the Missionaries of Charity. When she began it, she had no grand plan, no firm ideas about what would work and what wouldn't. "We started the work as the suffering of the people called us," Mother Teresa later explained. "God showed us what to do."

10   Donors helped by contributing buildings and other facilities. In 1952, for example, the city of Calcutta gave her a Kali temple. She turned the temple into the Niral Hriday (Pure Heart) Home for the Dying Destitutes. A few of the people who went there survived, but most did not. The home wasn't designed to cure sick people. Most were beyond medical

Mother Teresa receives the Doctor of Humane Letters from Georgetown University.

intervention. Rather, the home was "a shelter where the dying poor may die in dignity."

11 Mother Teresa's work attracted many other nuns who volunteered to help. But all had to take her fourth vow. All had to make poverty their chosen way of life. As Mother Teresa once said, "To be able to love the poor and know the poor we must be poor ourselves." Therefore, she added, "We cannot work for the rich; neither can we accept any money for what we do."

12 In 1964, Pope Paul VI came to visit Mother Teresa. He gave her his own white limousine. She never even bothered to take a ride in it. Instead, Mother Teresa sold the car and used the money to start a new colony for people suffering from leprosy.

13 Slowly, the Missionaries of Charity grew. At first, Mother Teresa and her nuns worked only in Calcutta. As their numbers grew, they opened up clinics and schools in other parts of India. By 1965, the order had spread overseas. By the 1990s, the order, which by then included men (called brothers), had grown to more than 4,500. They operated about 550 centers in 126 countries.

14 As Mother Teresa's order grew, so too did her fame. People around the world heaped honors upon her. In New York City, the mayor gave her the key to the city. Mother Teresa won the Pope John XXIII Peace Prize. India awarded her the Jewel of India, that nation's highest honor. And in 1979, Mother Teresa won the Nobel Peace Prize.

15 Not everyone loved Mother Teresa, however. Even she had critics. Some people attacked her because she didn't do enough to change the structure of society. It was fine to work with poor people, the critics said, but what about the causes of poverty? Shouldn't she do more about that? Shouldn't she perhaps lead a revolution?

16 No, Mother Teresa responded firmly, that was not her calling. "If people feel it is their vocation to change structure," she declared, "then that is the work they must do." Her job had always been to treat one tortured soul at a time.

17 Less than five feet tall, deeply wrinkled, and stooped over by hard work, Mother Teresa remained tough as nails. She never really retired, not even after suffering two heart attacks. Her doctors wanted her to take it easy, but as she once joked, "What doctor is going to tell Mother Teresa she has a bad heart?"

18 By 1996, her legendary strength was just about gone. Mother Teresa was in and out of the hospital several times. Her heart was weak, and she had trouble breathing. On September 5, 1997, she died.

19 Many people, looking back on Mother Teresa's life, praised this tireless and selfless woman and tried to find words that would sum up her life. But Mother Teresa had done it best herself when she said, "By blood and origin, I am an Albanian. My citizenship is Indian. I am a Catholic nun. As to my calling, I belong to the whole world."

If you have been timed while reading this article, enter your reading time below. Then turn to the Words-per-Minute Table on page 195 and look up your reading speed (words per minute). Enter your reading speed on the graph on page 196.

Reading Time: Lesson 20

_____ : _____
Minutes   *Seconds*

A | Finding the Main Idea

One statement below expresses the main idea of the article. One statement is too general, or too broad. The other statement explains only part of the article; it is too narrow. Label the statements using the following key:

M—Main Idea **B—Too Broad** **N—Too Narrow**

_____ 1. Mother Teresa dedicated her life to poor people.

_____ 2. After comforting a dying woman, Mother Teresa formed a new religious order called the Missionaries of Charity.

_____ 3. With great love and fierce determination, Mother Teresa served the poor and dying in India and around the world.

_____ Score 15 points for a correct M answer.

_____ Score 5 points for each correct B or N answer.

_____ **Total Score:** Finding the Main Idea

B | Recalling Facts

How well do you remember the facts in the article? Put an X in the box next to the answer that correctly completes each statement about the article.

1. In addition to the three sacred vows taken by all Catholic nuns, Mother Teresa took a fourth vow promising to
   ☐ a. remain poor.
   ☐ b. provide free service to the poor.
   ☐ c. remain unmarried.

2. During her first 20 years in India, Sister Teresa
   ☐ a. taught children living in the slums of Calcutta.
   ☐ b. founded a home where the dying poor could die in dignity.
   ☐ c. taught upper-class children in Calcutta.

3. Mother Teresa was given her name by the
   ☐ a. people under her care in the Niral Hriday Home for the Dying Destitutes.
   ☐ b. slum children she taught in Calcutta.
   ☐ c. children she taught at St. Mary's High School.

4. When Pope Paul VI gave Mother Teresa a white limousine, she
   ☐ a. sold it and used the money to start a new colony for people suffering from leprosy.
   ☐ b. took a ride in it.
   ☐ c. sold it and gave the money to the poor people of Calcutta.

5. India awarded Mother Teresa that nation's highest honor, the
   ☐ a. Pope John XXIII Peace Prize.
   ☐ b. Nobel Peace Prize.
   ☐ c. Jewel of India.

Score 5 points for each correct answer.

_____ **Total Score:** Recalling Facts

C | Making Inferences

When you combine your own experience and information from a text to draw a conclusion that is not directly stated in that text, you are making an inference. Below are five statements that may or may not be inferences based on information in the article. Label the statements using the following key:

C—Correct Inference   **F—Faulty Inference**

_____ 1. The people of India felt that Mother Teresa did not do enough for their country's poor.

_____ 2. Mother Teresa did not desire material possessions.

_____ 3. Mother Teresa eliminated poverty and cleaned up the slums in Calcutta.

_____ 4. The Missionaries of Charity joined the order so that they could become as famous as Mother Teresa.

_____ 5. Mother Teresa probably used the money she received from the Nobel Peace Prize to help fund her clinics and schools.

Score 5 points for each correct answer.

_____ **Total Score:** Making Inferences

D | Using Words Precisely

Each numbered sentence below contains an underlined word or phrase from the article. Following the sentence are three definitions. One definition is closest to the meaning of the underlined word. One definition is opposite or nearly opposite. Label those two definitions using the following key. Do not label the remaining definition.

C—Closest   **O—Opposite or Nearly Opposite**

1. She found such people in the <u>slums</u> of Calcutta, India.

_____ a. ghettos

_____ b. upper-class areas

_____ c. homes

2. The knowledge came to her as a divine <u>revelation</u>, which she later described as "a call within a call."

_____ a. something that is hidden from view

_____ b. prayer

_____ c. something that is disclosed by God

3. Right there, in that <u>festering</u> slum, Sister Teresa opened a new school.

_____ a. depressing

_____ b. thriving

_____ c. decaying

4. Mother Teresa's work attracted many other nuns who <u>volunteered</u> to help.

_____ a. willingly offered

_____ b. sadly witnessed

_____ c. absolutely refused

5. By 1996, her <u>legendary</u> strength was just about gone.

_____ a. obscure

_____ b. well known

_____ c. underdeveloped

_____ Score 3 points for each correct C answer.

_____ Score 2 points for each correct O answer.

_____ **Total Score:** Using Words Precisely

Enter the four total scores in the spaces below, and add them together to find your Reading Comprehension Score. Then record your score on the graph on page 197.

Score	Question Type	Lesson 20
_____	Finding the Main Idea	
_____	Recalling Facts	
_____	Making Inferences	
_____	Using Words Precisely	
_____	**Reading Comprehension Score**	

Author's Approach

Put an X in the box next to the correct answer.

1. What does the author mean by the statement "When the people of India called her the 'saint of the gutter,' they meant it as high praise"?

☐ a. The people of India criticized Mother Teresa for not doing enough to help the poor.

☐ b. The people of India greatly appreciated Mother Teresa's efforts to help the poor.

☐ c. Many people in India made fun of Mother Teresa and her work.

2. The main purpose of the first paragraph is to

☐ a. describe Mother Teresa's selflessness.

☐ b. compare Mother Teresa to other nuns.

☐ c. inform the reader about conditions in Calcutta, India.

3. From the statements below, choose those that you believe the author would agree with.

☐ a. Mother Teresa lived a saintly life.

☐ b. Mother Teresa should have done more to address the causes of poverty.

☐ c. The Indian people owe Mother Teresa a large debt of gratitude.

4. Choose the statement below that best describes the author's position in paragraph 16.

☐ a. Mother Teresa felt she had to defend herself against her critics.

☐ b. Mother Teresa was not upset by her critics because she was clear about her calling in life.

☐ c. Mother Teresa felt superior to those who criticized her.

_____ Number of correct answers

Record your personal assessment of your work on the Critical Thinking Chart on page 198.

CRITICAL THINKING

Summarizing and Paraphrasing

Put an X in the box next to the correct answer for question 2. Follow the directions provided for the other question.

1. Look for the important ideas and events in paragraphs 13 and 14. Summarize those paragraphs in one or two sentences.

_____

_____

_____

2. Choose the best one-sentence paraphrase for the following sentence from the article:
   "Her doctors wanted her to take it easy, but as she once joked, 'What doctor is going to tell Mother Teresa she has a bad heart?'"

   ☐ a. Mother Teresa joked about her heart disease because she didn't believe it was very serious.

   ☐ b. Mother Teresa joked that doctors didn't want to tell her she had a bad heart because she was such a loving person.

   ☐ c. Mother Teresa's doctors knew she was sick, but they were afraid to tell her so.

   _____ Number of correct answers

   Record your personal assessment of your work on the Critical Thinking Chart on page 198.

Critical Thinking

Put an X in the box next to the correct answer for questions 1, 2, and 4. Follow the directions provided for the other questions.

1. Which of the following statements from the article is an opinion rather than a fact?

   ☐ a. "Not everyone loved Mother Teresa."

   ☐ b. "'If people feel it is their vocation to change structure,' she declared, 'then that is the work they must do.'"

   ☐ c. "Even as a young girl growing up in Albania—where she was known as Agnes Bojaxhiu—this extraordinary individual knew her calling in life."

2. Based on what Mother Teresa said, you can predict that the men and women who had joined her order would

   ☐ a. continue to live with and serve the poor.

   ☐ b. begin trying to change the structure of society.

   ☐ c. accept money for their work.

3. Choose from the letters below to correctly complete the following statement. Write the letters on the lines.

   In the article, _____ and _____ are alike.

   a. the work performed by the Sisters of Loretto

   b. the work performed by Mother Teresa

   c. the work performed by the Missionaries of Charity

4. What was the cause of Mother Teresa's decision to leave St. Mary's?

☐ a. She realized her life's work after she had given comfort to a dying woman.

☐ b. The city of Calcutta gave her a Kali temple, which she could use to shelter the dying poor.

☐ c. She had a divine revelation, which instructed her to "follow Jesus into the slums."

5. In which paragraph did you find your information or details to answer question 4?

_____

_____ Number of correct answers

Record your personal assessment of your work on the Critical Thinking Chart on page 198.

Personal Response

This article is different from other stories about heroes I've read because

_____

_____

and Mother Teresa is unlike other heroes because

_____

_____

Self-Assessment

The part I found most difficult about the article was

_____

_____

_____

_____

I found this difficult because

_____

_____

_____

_____

HANS & SOPHIE SCHOLL
Resisting Nazi Terror

Hans and Sophie Scholl in Munich, Germany, during the summer of 1942

Hans and Sophie Scholl were ordinary children. They didn't plan on becoming heroes. Hans was born in 1918, and his sister Sophie in 1921. They spent their childhood playing in the fields of a small German town where their father was mayor. They were happy children and looked forward to a bright future. Their dreams were simple: Sophie wanted to be a kindergarten teacher, and Hans hoped to be a doctor. But life did not stay simple for Hans and Sophie. Germany was changing in the 1930s, and the changes were to alter the lives of both Sophie and Hans.

2   First came the rise of Adolf Hitler and the Nazi Party. Hitler promised to make Germany great. He promised to create new jobs, unite the German people, and restore pride in the fatherland. Those promises sounded so appealing that most people supported Hitler and his Nazi Party. But Hitler had other, less glorious goals that many people did not know about at first. He believed that the German people were the best and smartest on earth. And though that might sound like simple pride in his people, it was part

of a twisted view of humanity. It was coupled with a belief that everyone else was inferior, and that they should be controlled by the Germans. He also had an irrational hatred for certain people, the Jews in particular. He began an organized program to wipe all Jews from the face of the earth.

3   Hitler expected all Germans to agree with him. He wanted everyone to share his warped dream. To teach the German children his ideas, he set up an organization called the Hitler Youth. At first the organization seemed much like America's Boy Scouts and Girl Scouts. Troops of Hitler Youth sang songs, learned crafts, and took hikes through the German countryside. Soon, however, the leaders of the group demanded that all members become Nazis. Children in the organization were no longer allowed to sing their own songs or carry their own handmade flags. They could sing only Nazi songs and carry only Hitler's flag.

4   Like many young Germans, Sophie and Hans Scholl joined the Hitler Youth. But gradually they began to see the evil of the Nazi movement. They began to pull away from the group and to speak out against it. Because of his protests against the group, Hans was sent to prison for a little while in 1938. By that time the dark side of Hitler's plan was clear to both Hans and Sophie.

5   In 1939, Hans left for the University of Munich to study medicine. Sophie joined him in 1942 as a student of biology and philosophy. In Munich, the Scholls met others who hated what Hitler was doing. They learned that Hitler had set up concentration camps for Jews. Hitler's soldiers were rounding up all the Jews they could find and shipping them off to the camps, where they were starved, tortured, and killed. As Hans and Sophie talked with other students, they arrived at a decision: they had to do something to try to stop Hitler. They believed that any person who did not actively resist the Nazis had to share the guilt for Hitler's deeds. To do nothing was to allow the terror to continue.

6   And so the White Rose was born. Working with a few close friends, Hans and Sophie created the White Rose, a secret resistance group. Their goal was to spread the word of Hitler's crimes against the Jews and so rouse other students to protest. It was a dangerous undertaking. The Nazis would not tolerate any resistance. They would imprison or kill anyone who disagreed with their policies.

7   Nevertheless, Hans managed to get his hands on a printing press, and the group began their activities. Working at night in the basement of Hans and Sophie's apartment, they put together a series of four pamphlets called the *Leaflets of the White Rose*. Each leaflet urged the German people to rise up against Hitler.

8   It was dangerous enough to write and print the leaflets, but it was even more dangerous to distribute them. Nazi soldiers were positioned throughout the city and were free to stop anyone they

Hans Scholl (left) and Sophie Scholl at the railroad station in Munich, Germany, 1942

chose. Soldiers often demanded to be allowed to search a bag, a suitcase, or even a person's body. If anything suspicious was found, the person might be whisked off to a concentration camp for questioning and possible torture.

9   Despite the great risk involved, it was often Sophie or Hans who volunteered to pack a suitcase with leaflets and carry it out into the city. Sometimes Hans left leaflets in an empty classroom at the university. Sometimes Sophie moved quietly through the streets in the early morning hours, slipping one leaflet into each mailbox she passed. Sometimes Hans and Sophie even took trains to other cities in the hope that the resistance would spread beyond Munich.

10   The leaflets produced by the White Rose caused a lot of excitement at the university. In fact, throughout the city people began to whisper about the bold pamphlets. So as Sophie and Hans hoped, the resistance did spread to other cities. The leaflets were reprinted by students in Hamburg and eventually made their way to England, where they were copied by the thousands.

11   Meanwhile, the Nazis were moving in on the Scholls. February 18, 1943, was a beautiful sunny morning. Hans and Sophie left their apartment together and headed for the university. They had with them a suitcase full of the forbidden leaflets. They reached the university and quickly scattered the leaflets around the campus. But this time they were spotted, and within minutes the German police had arrested them both.

12   Hans and Sophie knew that the Nazis would probably show them no mercy. The White Rose was a symbol of freedom, and that was exactly what Hitler was trying to destroy. Thus Sophie was not surprised when the endless hours of questioning began. For two days and two nights, Sophie was grilled by Nazi officials. In a separate room, Hans was suffering the same treatment.

13   At first Sophie and Hans denied everything. But when it became clear that the Nazis had proof of their illegal actions, Sophie and Hans reversed their story. They took the blame for everything that the White Rose had done. They insisted that they were the only people who knew anything about the leaflets. Sophie and Hans were trying to protect the other members of the resistance group.

14   Confessing to the crimes was an act of courage. If the Scholls had denied the charges, or if they had given the names of other White Rose members, their lives might have been spared. But now the Nazis would surely put them to death. Still, Sophie and Hans remained calm, brave, and unwavering in their contempt for Hitler. The Nazi officials had never seen anything like it. Not once did Sophie or Hans apologize or ask for forgiveness.

They believed in their cause. Their spirits could not be broken.

15   On Sunday afternoon, three days after the arrest, the Nazis stopped questioning the Scholls. The police had made their decision. Hans and Sophie would be executed the very next day. With death only a few hours away, the Scholls still retained their composure. They both slept soundly that night, for their consciences were clear. Sophie and Hans had not stopped Hitler, but their actions had helped awaken the world to his crimes.

16   When Sophie walked to the executioner's block the next day, she held her head high. She died quietly, with dignity. Her brother Hans showed similar courage. His final words before the ax fell were, "Long live freedom!"

If you have been timed while reading this article, enter your reading time below. Then turn to the Words-per-Minute Table on page 195 and look up your reading speed (words per minute). Enter your reading speed on the graph on page 196.

Reading Time: Lesson 21

_____ : _____

Minutes   Seconds

A | Finding the Main Idea

One statement below expresses the main idea of the article. One statement is too general, or too broad. The other statement explains only part of the article; it is too narrow. Label the statements using the following key:

M—Main Idea   **B—Too Broad**   **N—Too Narrow**

_____ 1. Sophie and Hans Scholl were German students who distributed many leaflets against the Nazis.

_____ 2. Sophie and Hans Scholl acted with great courage and conviction in an effort to educate the world about the Nazis.

_____ 3. Sophie and Hans Scholl were German students who risked their lives and finally died trying to alert the world to the evils of Adolf Hitler.

_____ Score 15 points for a correct M answer.

_____ Score 5 points for each correct B or N answer.

_____ **Total Score:** Finding the Main Idea

B | Recalling Facts

How well do you remember the facts in the article? Put an X in the box next to the answer that correctly completes each statement about the article.

1. As children, Hans and Sophie Scholl were
   - ☐ a. members of the Hitler Youth.
   - ☐ b. members of the Boy Scouts and Girl Scouts.
   - ☐ c. unhappy living in Germany.

2. The leaflets of the White Rose were printed in
   - ☐ a. a classroom at the University of Munich.
   - ☐ b. the basement of the Scholls' apartment.
   - ☐ c. Hans and Sophie's hometown.

3. Members of the White Rose sometimes distributed leaflets by
   - ☐ a. mailing them to students in other cities.
   - ☐ b. handing them out to people on street corners.
   - ☐ c. slipping them into mailboxes.

4. When captured, Sophie and Hans took responsibility for printing the leaflets because they
   - ☐ a. wanted to protect the other members of the White Rose.
   - ☐ b. were afraid of being tortured.
   - ☐ c. were hoping the Nazis would be merciful.

5. Four days after Hans and Sophie were arrested,
   - ☐ a. Sophie finally gave police the names of all White Rose members.
   - ☐ b. they apologized for what they had done.
   - ☐ c. they were executed.

Score 5 points for each correct answer.

_____ **Total Score:** Recalling Facts

C Making Inferences

When you combine your own experience and information from a text to draw a conclusion that is not directly stated in that text, you are making an inference. Below are five statements that may or may not be inferences based on information in the article. Label the statements using the following key:

C—Correct Inference   **F—Faulty Inference**

_____ 1. The other members of the White Rose were eventually caught and executed too.

_____ 2. Sophie and Hans volunteered to distribute the leaflets because they liked taking risks.

_____ 3. The execution of Hans and Sophie ended all resistance to Hitler in Germany.

_____ 4. Sophie and Hans were more interested in standing up for their ideals than they were in saving their own lives.

_____ 5. Nazi officials expected their prisoners to break down and beg for mercy.

Score 5 points for each correct answer.

_____ **Total Score:** Making Inferences

D Using Words Precisely

Each numbered sentence below contains an underlined word or phrase from the article. Following the sentence are three definitions. One definition is closest to the meaning of the underlined word. One definition is opposite or nearly opposite. Label those two definitions using the following key. Do not label the remaining definition.

C—Closest   **O—Opposite or Nearly Opposite**

1. They believed that any person who did not actively <u>resist</u> the Nazis had to share the guilt for Hitler's deeds.

_____ a. escape from

_____ b. express disapproval of

_____ c. support

2. Their goal was to spread the word of Hitler's crimes against the Jews and so <u>rouse</u> other students to protest.

_____ a. excite

_____ b. soothe

_____ c. force

3. The Nazis would not <u>tolerate</u> any resistance.

_____ a. forbid

_____ b. allow

_____ c. expect

4. Still, Sophie and Hans remained calm, brave, and <u>unwavering</u> in their contempt for Hitler.

_____ a. angry

_____ b. uncertain

_____ c. steady

5. With death only a few hours away, the Scholls still retained their <u>composure</u>.

_____ a. self-control

_____ b. religious convictions

_____ c. nervousness

_____ Score 3 points for each correct C answer.

_____ Score 2 points for each correct O answer.

_____ **Total Score:** Using Words Precisely

Enter the four total scores in the spaces below, and add them together to find your Reading Comprehension Score. Then record your score on the graph on page 197.

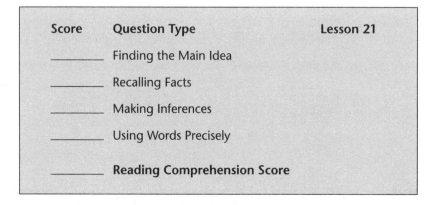

Score	Question Type	Lesson 21
_____	Finding the Main Idea	
_____	Recalling Facts	
_____	Making Inferences	
_____	Using Words Precisely	
_____	**Reading Comprehension Score**	

Author's Approach

Put an X in the box next to the correct answer.

1. The main purpose of the first paragraph is to

☐ a. convey a mood about the changes taking place in Germany.

☐ b. compare the childhood dreams of Hans and Sophie Scholl.

☐ c. express an opinion about Nazism and the rise of Hitler.

2. Which of the following statements from the article best describes Hans and Sophie Scholl?

☐ a. "Hans and Sophie Scholl were ordinary children."

☐ b. "Still, Sophie and Hans remained calm, brave, and unwavering in their contempt for Hitler."

☐ c. "Like many young Germans, Sophie and Hans Scholl joined the Hitler Youth."

3. What does the author imply by saying "But Hitler had other, less glorious goals that many people did not know about at first"?

☐ a. Hitler did not want the German people to know about some of the things he had done in the past.

☐ b. The German people didn't care what Hitler did as long as he created new jobs and fulfilled other important goals.

☐ c. Hitler did not reveal his horrible plans for the Jews until he had gained the support of the German people.

4. Choose the statement below that best describes the author's position in paragraph 14.

☐ a. Hans and Sophie were so committed to their cause that they were willing to die for it.

☐ b. The other White Rose members deserted Hans and Sophie and let them face the Nazi officials alone.

☐ c. The Nazis were monsters who did not tolerate any opposition.

_____ Number of correct answers

Record your personal assessment of your work on the Critical Thinking Chart on page 198.

Summarizing and Paraphrasing

Put an X in the box next to the correct answer for question 2. Follow the directions provided for the other question.

1. Complete the following one-sentence summary of the article using the lettered phrases from the phrase bank below. Write the letters on the lines.

Phrase Bank:
a. their gradual rejection of the Nazi movement
b. their capture and execution by the Nazis
c. their efforts to actively resist the Nazis

The article about Hans and Sophie Scholl begins with _____, goes on to explain _____, and ends with _____.

2. Read the following statement about the article. Then read the paraphrase of that statement. Choose the reason that best tells why the paraphrase does not say the same thing as the statement.

Statement: After Hans and Sophie Scholl distributed the *Leaflets of the White Rose,* people throughout Munich read them in amazement because opposition to the Nazi movement was unusual.

Paraphrase: Hans and Sophie Scholl spread the word about their resistance movement to the people of Munich.

☐ a. Paraphrase says too much.

☐ b. Paraphrase doesn't say enough.

☐ c. Paraphrase doesn't agree with the statement about the article.

_____ Number of correct answers

Record your personal assessment of your work on the Critical Thinking Chart on page 198.

Critical Thinking

Put an X in the box next to the correct answer for questions 2, 4, and 5. Follow the directions provided for the other questions.

1. For each statement below, write O if it expresses an opinion and write F if it expresses a fact.

_____ a. The German people are the best and smartest on earth.

_____ b. Adolf Hitler believed that the Jews were inferior.

_____ c. The Scholls risked their lives to distribute the White Rose leaflets.

CRITICAL THINKING

2. Based on the information in paragraph 15, you can predict that

☐ a. the other members of the White Rose would leave Munich.

☐ b. others would continue to rise up against Hitler.

☐ c. Hitler would be stopped by the other members of the White Rose.

3. Think about cause–effect relationships in the article. Fill in the blanks in the cause–effect chart, drawing from the letters below.

Cause	Effect
The Scholls took leaflets to other cities.	_____
_____	The police arrested the Scholls.
Hans and Sophie confessed to their crimes.	_____

a. Hans and Sophie were seen distributing leaflets in the university.

b. The pamphlets were reprinted and made their way to England.

c. The Scholls were executed.

4. How are Hans and Sophie examples of heroes?

☐ a. They died with dignity.

☐ b. They actively resisted a powerful evil.

☐ c. They confessed their crimes against the Nazis.

5. What did you have to do to answer question 2?

☐ a. find an opinion (what someone thinks about something)

☐ b. find an effect (something that happened)

☐ c. draw a conclusion (a sensible statement based on the text and your experience)

_____ Number of correct answers

Record your personal assessment of your work on the Critical Thinking Chart on page 198.

Personal Response

What would you have done when the Nazis' purpose became clear?

_____

_____

_____

_____

Self-Assessment

One good question about this article that was not asked would be

_____

_____

_____

and the answer is

_____

_____

_____

CRITICAL THINKING

Compare and Contrast

Think about the articles you have read in Unit Three. Write the names of the three heroes you admired the most in the first column of the chart below. Use information you learned from the articles to fill in the empty boxes in the chart.

My Hero	What challenge did this hero meet?	Why is what this hero did important today?	What would you have done in the same situation?

Suppose two of the heroes you read about in this unit met one another. What might they talk about? On the lines below write a conversation you think the two might have.

_____

_____

_____

_____

_____

Words-per-Minute Table

Unit Three

Directions: If you were timed while reading an article, refer to the Reading Time you recorded in the box at the end of the article. Use this words-per-minute table to determine your reading speed for that article. Then plot your reading speed on the graph on page 196.

Lesson No. of Words	15 961	16 1351	17 1017	18 1383	19 1261	20 1198	21 1274	
1:30	641	901	678	922	841	799	849	**90**
1:40	577	811	610	830	757	719	764	**100**
1:50	524	737	555	754	688	653	695	**110**
2:00	481	676	509	692	631	599	637	**120**
2:10	444	624	469	638	582	553	588	**130**
2:20	412	579	436	593	540	513	546	**140**
2:30	384	540	407	553	504	479	510	**150**
2:40	360	507	381	519	473	449	478	**160**
2:50	339	477	359	488	445	423	450	**170**
3:00	320	450	339	461	420	399	425	**180**
3:10	303	427	321	437	398	378	402	**190**
3:20	288	405	305	415	378	359	382	**200**
3:30	275	386	291	395	360	342	364	**210**
3:40	262	368	277	377	344	327	347	**220**
3:50	251	352	265	361	329	313	332	**230**
4:00	240	338	254	346	315	300	319	**240**
4:10	231	324	244	332	303	288	306	**250**
4:20	222	312	235	319	291	276	294	**260**
4:30	214	300	226	307	280	266	283	**270**
4:40	206	290	218	296	270	257	273	**280**
4:50	199	280	210	286	261	248	264	**290**
5:00	192	270	203	277	252	240	255	**300**
5:10	186	261	197	268	244	232	247	**310**
5:20	180	253	191	259	236	225	239	**320**
5:30	175	246	185	251	229	218	232	**330**
5:40	170	238	179	244	223	211	225	**340**
5:50	165	232	174	237	216	205	218	**350**
6:00	160	225	170	231	210	200	212	**360**
6:10	156	219	165	224	204	194	207	**370**
6:20	152	213	161	218	199	189	201	**380**
6:30	148	208	156	213	194	184	196	**390**
6:40	144	203	153	207	189	180	191	**400**
6:50	141	198	149	202	185	175	186	**410**
7:00	137	193	145	198	180	171	182	**420**
7:10	134	189	142	193	176	167	178	**430**
7:20	131	184	139	189	172	163	174	**440**
7:30	128	180	136	184	168	160	170	**450**
7:40	125	176	133	180	164	156	166	**460**
7:50	123	172	130	176	161	153	163	**470**
8:00	120	169	127	173	158	150	159	**480**

Minutes and Seconds

Seconds

Plotting Your Progress: Reading Speed

Unit Three

Directions: If you were timed while reading an article, write your words-per-minute rate for that article in the box under the number of the lesson. Then plot your reading speed on the graph by putting a small X on the line directly above the number of the lesson, across from the number of words per minute you read. As you mark your speed for each lesson, graph your progress by drawing a line to connect the X's.

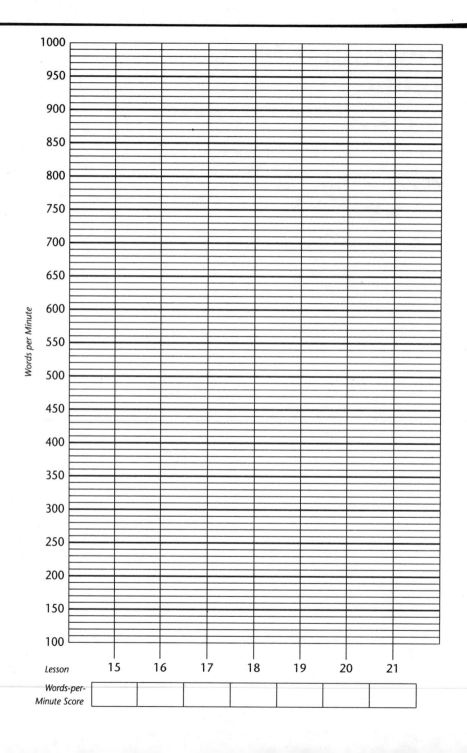

Words per Minute

Lesson   15   16   17   18   19   20   21

Words-per-Minute Score							

Plotting Your Progress: Reading Comprehension

Unit Three

Directions: Write your Reading Comprehension score for each lesson in the box under the number of the lesson. Then plot your score on the graph by putting a small X on the line directly above the number of the lesson and across from the score you earned. As you mark your score for each lesson, graph your progress by drawing a line to connect the X's.

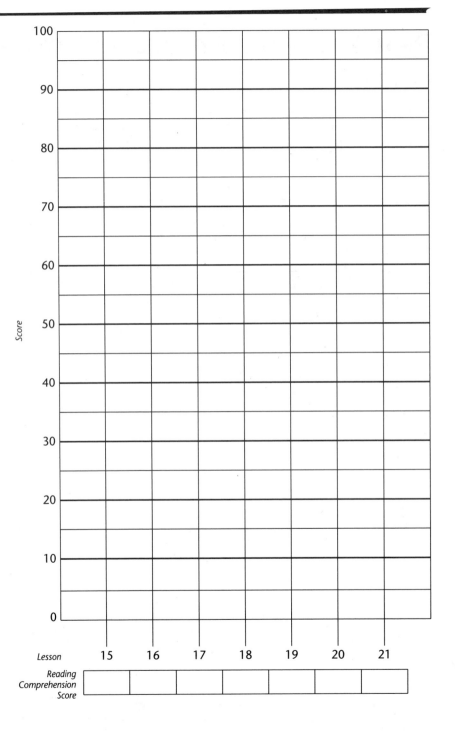

Plotting Your Progress: Critical Thinking

Unit Three

Directions: Work with your teacher to evaluate your responses to the Critical Thinking questions for each lesson. Then fill in the appropriate spaces in the chart below. For each lesson and each type of Critical Thinking question, do the following: Mark a minus sign (–) in the box to indicate areas in which you feel you could improve. Mark a plus sign (+) to indicate areas in which you feel you did well. Mark a minus-slash-plus sign (–/+) to indicate areas in which you had mixed success. Then write any comments you have about your performance, including ideas for improvement.

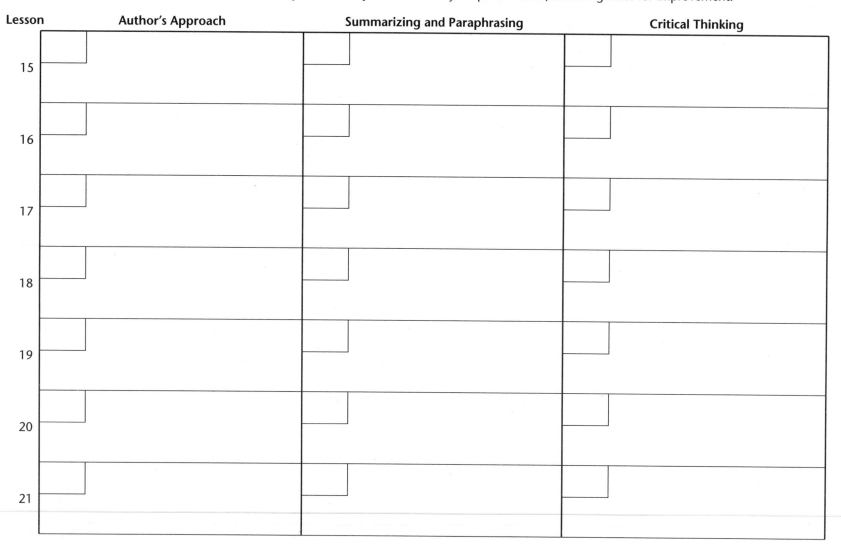

Lesson	Author's Approach	Summarizing and Paraphrasing	Critical Thinking
15			
16			
17			
18			
19			
20			
21			

Picture Credits

Cover: With permission of the Institute of Heraldry, Department of the Army

Sample Lesson: p. 3, 4 Charles Periera, U.S. Park Police/AP/Wide World Photos; p. 5 AP/Wide World Photos

Unit 1 Opener: p. 13 Nathan Bilow/All-Sport USA

Lesson 1: pp. 14, 15 AP/Wide World Photos

Lesson 2: pp. 22, 23 Nathan Bilow/All-Sport USA

Lesson 3: p. 30 AP/Wide World Photos; p. 31 UPI/Corbis-Bettmann

Lesson 4: p. 38 Russell Thompson/Archive Photos; p. 39 From *The Small Woman,* by Alan Burgess, Copyright 1957, by E.P. Dutton, Inc. Reprinted by permission of the publisher.

Lesson 5: pp.46, 47 UPI/Corbis-Bettmann

Lesson 6: p. 54 Paul Hurschmann/AP/Wide World Photos; p. 55 U.S. Holocaust Memorial Museum/ © Anne Frank Foundation/AFS-Amsterdam, The Netherlands

Lesson 7: p. 62 AP/Wide World Photos; p. 63 Dinodia/The Image Works

Unit 2 Opener: p. 75 "The Halt for Lunch in Last Forced March" from *The North Pole—Its Discovery in 1909 Under the Auspices of the Peary Arctic Club,* by Robert E. Peary, Copyright 1910 by Frederick A. Stokes Co. (Greenwood Press, Copyright 1968)

Lesson 8: p. 76 "The Halt for Lunch in Last Forced March" from *The North Pole—Its Discovery in 1909 Under the Auspices of the Peary Arctic Club,* by Robert E. Peary, Copyright 1910 by Frederick A. Stokes Co. (Greenwood Press, Copyright 1968); p. 77 Corbis-Bettmann

Lesson 9: p. 84 (L) Berg/Greenpeace (R) Davis/Greenpeace; p. 85 Paul Latoures/The Goldman Environmental Foundation

Lesson 10: p. 92 Original illustration by Tanya Rosburg, based on similiar illustrations in the Lindbergh Historical Site Instructor's Guide, complied by Lori Nelson and published in 1982 by the Minnesota Historical Society. (from *Charles A. Lindbergh, A Bio-Bibliography* by Perry D. Luckett, Copyright 1986, Greenwood Press, Inc.); p. 93 Brown Brothers

Lesson 11: p. 100 Alain Nogues/Sygma; p. 101 AP/Wide World Photos

Lesson 12: p. 108 AP/Wide World Photos; p. 109 John F. Burns/New York Times Co./Archive Photos

Lesson 13: p. 116 Danny Johnston/AP/Wide World Photos; p. 117 UPI/Corbis-Bettmann

Lesson 14: p. 124 Archive Photos; p. 125 Agence France Presse/Corbis-Bettmann

Unit 3 Opener: 137 James Kubus/*PetLife* Magazine

Lesson 15: p. 138 Douglas Clifford/St. Louis Post-Dispatch; p. 139 Ted Dargen/St. Louis Post-Dispatch

Lesson 16: p. 146 UPI/Corbis-Bettmann; p. 147 New York Police Department

Lesson 17: p. 154 Corbis-Bettmann; p. 155 Brown Brothers

Lesson 18: p. 162 James Kubus/*PetLife* Magazine; p. 163 Robert F. Bukaty/AP/Wide World Photos

Lesson 19: pp. 170, 171 Corbis-Bettmann

Lesson 20: p. 178 UPI/Corbis-Bettmann; p. 179 J.C. Francolon/Gamma-Liaison

Lesson 21: pp. 186, 187 George J. Wittenstein, United States Holocaust Memorial Museum